BILLY BEAUMONT

D0676105

BILLY BEAUMONT
The Lion of Winter

Sean Pryor

A STAR BOOK
Published by
the Paperback Division of
W. H. ALLEN & Co. Ltd

A Star Book
Published in 1983
by the Paperback Division of
W. H. Allen & Co. Ltd
A Howard and Wyndham Company
44 Hill Street, London W1X 8LB

Copyright © 1983 by Sean Pryor

Printed and bound in Great Britain by
Cox & Wyman Ltd, Reading

ISBN 0 352 31233 5

CONTENTS

For Bill and Pat Pryor

PROLOGUE

For a sudden second, the waving banners died in the breeze and the wall of sound fell away to silence. In the middle of the pitch, a knot of players in hooped and quartered shirts huddled anxiously around the tall man in the white headband as he struggled to focus on their pale faces. Then, with a sad shake of the head, he signalled to the anxious watchers on the sidelines and began to trudge towards the dressing room. The silence became a rumble and then an ovation as the player, now supported by coach and physiotherapist, walked on. The career of Billy Beaumont was at an end.

All afternoon, the historic Reddings ground in the industrial Midlands near Birmingham had witnessed the ebb and flow of battle as Lancashire, commemorating their centenary, had struggled for the prize that would crown their celebrations. Their opponents, North Midlands, had repulsed every attack and under their shrewd captain, Les Cusworth, had come close to upsetting the favourites on a number of occasions. It was against this rugged background that Beaumont urged his men on in the only way he understood — by example. For the umpteenth time in the game he went down with the ball and found himself trapped at the bottom of a ruck. As arms and boots and elbows flew, he felt a sharp crack on the base of his skull. The pain was momentary. He shook his head to clear it and as play moved away, he got quickly to his feet and followed the ball.

Lancashire were gaining the initiative. Slowly their forward strength began to tell and now they had a real chance with a line out near the North Midlands 22. Beaumont ran to join it, taking up his customary place at number 2, ready to jump high and set his threequarters away with a clean, fast ball. But as he stood, waiting for the hooker's signal, the faces in the crowd and the player with the ball began to merge. Everything had become flat and one-dimensional. He shook his head again but the distortion persisted.

He remembered the blow on the back of the head minutes earlier and called on the Lancashire physiotherapist, Kevin Murphy, to examine him. They agreed that if the condition did not clear within a few minutes, the captain would have to come off. His team mates looked across anxiously. Beaumont was the one player they couldn't afford to lose.

The game surged on with Lancashire still calling the play until the dramatic moment when Beaumont stopped, looked around and decided he could not go on. In the cramped press box, the rugby writers consulted watches and compared notes. It was thirty-seven minutes into the first half, they agreed. 'Concussion,' some concluded, 'What bad luck . . .' But many of them suspected that the small story they would write that night would soon be a big one and dominate talk in rugby circles for weeks to come. Beaumont, they agreed, had taken one knock too many.

In the sanctuary of the dressing room, the England captain slumped down on a bench and closed his eyes. The Lancashire doctor came in to examine him, and then his wife appeared. Finally, a specialist who was at the ground joined them. His diagnosis was 'lack of visual discrimination', not concussion. It was more serious.

Half time had come and gone and his team, resigned now to his absence, began to step up the tempo. By the time their captain, refreshed by a steaming hot bath, walked out to the tunnel to watch the closing moments, they were in the lead with an unconverted try. Then in injury time they sealed their centenary win with a penalty. For Beaumont, the result was immensely satisfying, but he was in no mood to join the celebrations and instead went quietly home to rest. Familiar symptoms had appeared – tingling sensations in his tongue, pins and needles down his left side and an inability to speak coherently for any length of time. He slept fitfully.

The next morning, he was due in Manchester at the BBC Television studios to record a round in the panel game, *A Question of Sport*. He still felt ill but he managed to get through the show, leading his team to a win over Willy Carson's side. Later that day he made an appointment to see a neurological specialist who knew his case history well. The meeting was on the Monday and from the moment he arrived for work at the family textile business of Joseph Blackledge and Sons to be confronted by anxious pressmen, things began to move with lightning speed. 'Was he retiring?' they wanted to know. 'Not on your life', came the response. But in the back of his mind, there were nagging doubts. He recalled that in a career that began with Fylde in 1971, he had been concussed more than twenty times in the following five years. He broke it down into simple statistics – three or four injuries a year for six seasons.

The neurologist began a series of tests and made his conclusions, but referred Beaumont to another specialist for a second opinion. Again he underwent tests, brain scans figuring prominently. It took five hours and with each test he grew in confidence. Finally, he faced the surgeon for the final diagnosis. There would be no long term problems, the doctor told him. Beaumont relaxed. 'But,' he added gravely, 'you would be extremely foolish if you ever played rugby again.' There it was. The news he had dreaded, presented starkly and unequivocally. His days as captain of England, Lancashire, and the British Lions, were over. His world had collapsed.

Once the news was released, it seemed as though the whole of British rugby was in a state of shock. Friends, colleagues, press, administrators . . . all called to sympathise and remind him of his wonderful achievements. Tributes poured in from opponents and the public responded with sackfuls of mail. Beaumont in his reign as England player and captain had become a cult figure: like Henry Cooper, Bobby Charlton and Lester Piggot, he had progressed from obscurity to become a national institution. He had led English rugby out of the doldrums and given it triumphs to feast on. His progress 'through the ranks' was a triumph of courage and dedication and his story so surprising it might have been culled from the pages of a *Boy's Own* comic.

AN UNPROMISING START

The man who was destined to guide England's rugby fortunes through the promise of the late seventies to the glory of the early eighties was so sickly a baby that he nearly didn't make it to the family home near Chorley, much less to Twickenham.

His mother had had a difficult pregnancy and as time approached for the birth of her second child the doctors agreed that it would be safer to deliver by Caesarean section. In the fifties, that in itself was considered traumatic and potentially risky. But risks must be balanced and there was general relief in the Beaumont household when the baby was not only safely delivered a month ahead of time but weighed in at a lusty nine pounds. The date was March 9, 1952, and William Blackledge Beaumont – Blackledge after his paternal grandfather, founder of the family textile business – was the first son for Ron and Joyce. The eldest child was Alison, born eighteen months previously, who was always to be very close to Billy while brother Joe was to be born four years later.

All seemed well in the first few days but then came the first of several setbacks. Billy developed pneumonia, a highly dangerous condition in an infant, and there were real fears for his survival. Drugs to effectively combat the condition were rare, and in any case, highly experimental, but the Beaumonts were fortunate to have a skilled and thoughtful paediatrician in Dr Hesling and he moved heaven and earth to gain permission to use a new and still unproven drug on the youngster, called

Chloromycetin. Billy rallied, though the two weeks it took for the infection to decline must have been the most harrowing of Ron and Joyce Beaumont's lives.

Preparations for a triumphal homecoming began but a second, equally alarming setback occurred. The youngster was unable to retain his food and by the third week his weight had declined alarmingly from nine pounds to six pounds. This was symptomatic of a rare condition known as pyloric stenosis. It had occurred more than once in the Beaumont family cycle and Billy recalls that his uncle was one of the first babies born with the condition to survive. Basically, it describes a physical state where the exit of the stomach is so narrow that little or no food can pass through and can therefore not be properly digested. The stomach cannot retain the food and finally expels it through vomiting. It is, of course, a condition that can be cured by surgery, but a three-week old baby is by no means an ideal candidate for such a drastic course of action. Billy remembers that his uncle's survival was remarkable simply because his parents were totally resolute and infinitely patient. Billy's grandmother fed the child for the first year of its life with a liquid diet from a spoon no bigger than a farthing, and as it grew in strength its body developed to the point where it could ultimately manage for itself. In Billy's case it was decided that surgery was essential and the outcome was wholly successful.

That should be the end of a chequered medical history, but it wasn't. Billy continued to tax his anxious parents to the full by suddenly developing a septic condition and more intensive care was needed before he finally pulled through. That hurdle safely negotiated, Dr Hesling concluded the safest place for the youngster would be with his parents at home, and so finally, the village of Adlington was able to welcome the newest member of its fraternity.

The youngster had showed a healthy instinct for

2

survival so that the other two setbacks, asthma and a pigeon chest, became minor irritants rather than cause for concern. Billy recalls his father scrupulously carrying out a series of exercises designed to develop his chest, and to such effect, that by the time he was two, he looked remarkably like a pupil from the Charles Atlas school of bodybuilders rather than the puny 'seven stone weakling' he initially showed all promise of becoming. As for the asthma, that cleared up by itself as such childhood ailments frequently do. By the time he was eight years old and ready for boarding school, Billy Beaumont was a normal, healthy boy, already showing natural sporting aptitude with a penchant for soccer and a keen eye for cricket.

He certainly had the right pedigree for the latter. His uncle, Joe Blackledge, was captain of Lancashire County Cricket Club in the early sixties, and Billy recalls being taken to watch the team in action whenever they decamped from Old Trafford to the seaside at Blackpool. He was deeply impressed and his first modest ambition was not to score the winning goal in the cup final at Wembley, nor lead out England's rugby team at Twickenham, but to open the batting for the England cricket team at Lords, preferably opposite that staunch Yorkshireman, Geoffrey Boycott.

The boarding school his parents had chosen for him was a prep school called Cressbrook in Kirkby Lonsdale. It had a fine sporting tradition, a good academic standing and a penchant for physical discipline that manifested itself in ice cold baths each morning and interminable cross country walks on weekend afternoons. Its glittering sporting (and academic) star was John Spencer who, like Billy, would not only play for England and become a member of the British Lions, but captain his country as well.

It was at Cressbrook that Billy first began to play

rugby on a regular basis. Up until then, he and his pals had played soccer at every opportunity. It didn't need any organisation or even a proper pitch, just a couple of coats for goalposts and any ball ranging in size from a tennis ball to a beach ball. Best of all, it was a game you could just go out and get on with, a quality that appeals particularly to impatient, energetic seven-year-olds. And like most youngsters he had a soccer team to identify with, Blackburn Rovers, whose leading lights included such stars as Ronnie Clayton, the England captain, and Bryan Douglas. He remembers his first trip to a major sporting event was an excursion to Wembley to watch a soccer international. England put nine goals past the auld enemy, Scotland, a post war classic that many of us would have given our eye teeth to be present at. It made a deep impression. But so too did rugby when he was finally given an opportunity to demonstrate that his natural aptitude for sport embraced handling as much as kicking. He fancied himself as a fly half but, initially, he had to accept that his size made him an obvious candidate for the forwards. He began his illustrious career as a prop, a position he was to occupy with temporary distinction for Fylde and even for England in Australia when Mike Burton was sent off in the battle of Queensland.

In his second season at Cressbrook he managed to convince the games' master that, big or not, he was a creator not a destroyer and so, for three seasons, William Blackledge Beaumont starred at outside half for his school. He even became captain, a distinction that would be repeated only when he replaced Roger Uttley as skipper of the England side in 1978. A broken ankle limited his appearances and as a broken leg (incurred playing soccer on a tennis court!) followed soon afterwards, he found few opportunities to display early qualities of leadership. But while he thrived on the rough and tumble of winter sports, his great love remained cricket and he

4

was a useful opening batsman in the school first eleven.

After four happy years at Cressbrook, he was finally able to forgo the cold baths and cross country walks when he entered the more civilised environment of Ellesmere College in Shropshire. His career as a fly half continued through the under fourteen, under fifteen and under sixteen sides until finally, the rugby coach concluded his future lay elsewhere – at full back! And that is where he remained for two undistinguished seasons while he grew stronger and heavier and, inevitably, slower.

Despite his diffidence, he was a successful enough student to gain a sprinkling of 'O' Levels and it was only his lack of interest in matters academic that persuaded his father to let him leave before 'A' Levels beckoned. It was already clear that he would be needed in the family textile business, which, even in the late sixties, was undergoing radical changes as overseas competition decimated the industry and the need for innovation in technology and marketing became apparent. No pressure was put on him, but he was more than happy to go along with his father's wishes and take a diploma course in business studies and textile technology at a further education college. They chose Salford which seemed to prize sporting excellence as much as academic distinction. It was a happy and frutiful period in his development. Cricket received particular attention and he became a regular in the competitive Northern League, playing for Chorley alongside the equally gifted Paul Mariner, later to star for Ipswich and England as a prolific, goal-scoring forward. They became firm friends and remain so to this day.

As for rugby, he played for the College on Wednesdays and made his first tentative steps on the club ladder with Fylde on Saturdays, maintaining a connection that had begun with his grandfather and been continued through his father. By now, though,

5

all ambitions of being a successful back were fast receding. He was too big and too slow, so it was no surprise that after a brief flirtation with the full back position, he was politely asked to join the 'donkeys' and it was as a flanker in the sixth fifteen that the career of Billy Beaumont, captain of England and the British Lions, at last began to take shape.

MAKING THE GRADE

Fylde has never been one of England's most
fashionable clubs. It is a first class side, to be sure,
but tending towards the second division. On the other
hand, it is one of the happiest and best organised in
the land, and no slouch at promoting talent once
unearthed. Billy's talent was not immediately
apparent to the club selection committees.

He faced the problem many had faced before him
and do so to this day. He was too valuable to the
Coarse Rugby fraternity to be lost to the colours, and
so, whenever there was the slightest danger of a
selector from one of the higher sides seeing him play
well, his colleagues adopted a blissfully simple
approach. They starved him of the ball. It is hard to
make an impression when all you are allowed to do is
run around looking keen and hopeful. He languished
in the sixth team. His big break, if that is the word,
came when the third fifteen found themselves short
for a trip to Percy Park and the young man was
invited to join them. It was an excursion that Billy
recalls fondly. They won the game, he played well and
was introduced to the perils and delights of apres ski
in a way he had never dreamed of before. Instead of
returning to the bosom of his family the same
evening, as he had promised his worried mother, he
decamped to the family home in the late hours of the
following morning, not entirely sober. His mother
declared his rugby career at an end there and then,
but the intervening weeks softened her attitude and
Billy was restored to the Fylde fraternity not as the

sixth team flanker, but as lock forward in the seconds. It was, he remembers, Christmas 1969 when he took up for the first time the position which was to occupy most of his playing life.

By now, he was not only enjoying his rugby to the full, but he had become ambitious as well. He took up weight training and his strength made him a candidate for the front row where the first fifteen was less than formidable. After a schooling period back in the thirds, he made his first team debut against Waterloo in November 1970, and within two years, became not only an established member of the senior side, but also a county player with Lancashire.

By now he had stopped growing but was no longer short enough to be an effective prop. His height unbalanced the front row and so he concentrated on lock, a position which confirmed his natural ability as a jumper and a catcher, though usually at the front of the lineout rather than the 'glamour' position in the middle. He made his debut for Lancashire after only one full season in the first fifteen, at Fylde, against Cumberland and Westmorland in 1972. The match was won 13-0.

It was at this point that he came under the influence of Richard Trickey, one of the truly great characters in rugby football, who taught him many of the subtleties of second row play. Trickey nursed him so successfully in those early, hesitant days in a star-studded county side, that Billy was an automatic selection when the county toured South Africa and Rhodesia in 1974, his first overseas trip. He developed so well on that tour that on his return his second representative honour quickly followed. Tonga were touring Britain that autumn and Beaumont was chosen for the North of England side to play the visitors at Birkenhead Park, a week before the England under twenty-three side would meet them at Twickenham. Again he played well, and suddenly, he found himself selected as a reserve for the England game. His career was taking off at a bewildering pace.

Tonga were not a particularly formidable side. They played their rugby with the joy and abandon that might be expected of South Seas islanders. It won them many friends but hardly produced good results. England's aspiring internationals gave them a due roasting at Twickenham, but just after half time, they suffered an injury to their Number 8, Trevor Cheeseman, and a substitute was signalled for. Mal Malik, the Coventry flanker, was officially understudying the back row, but the selectors also had in their side Neil Mantell, the Rosslyn Park player who was equally talented at lock or Number 8. They decided to move Mantell out of the second row to replace Cheeseman at Number 8 and so, out on the pitch at a little after four o'clock on a dull afternoon, sprinted Billy Beaumont – wearing the white jersey of England for the very first time.

He played well, though with limited opportunities. Yet he made enough of an impression on the selectors to be called up for the series of regional trials that preceded the international season. It was at Headingley that Roger Uttley and he joined forces in the second row for the first time. Uttley was by then a senior international and established as a potent front line jumper. The selection had Billy in the middle of the line at Number 4 where he would oppose the outstanding England lock Nigel Horton. It was a prospect he didn't particularly relish. Horton was so much more experienced that the young Fylde player could expect a torrid and fruitless afternoon. But his Lancashire colleague Fran Cotton, who was to captain the Northern side, was alive to the problem. He suggested to Uttley that Beaumont's cause would be advanced if they were to switch positions, and to his delighted surprise Uttley agreed. The North won 28-13 and Beaumont had an impressive match. It was enough to get him into the junior side for the final trial at Twickenham where this time he would be opposing Uttley rather than partnering him. The senior side duly won, 38-22, and Beaumont was sure his career had taken a giant leap backwards. But again the selectors spotted something they liked. He was named for the squad of thirty from which the England team to play Ireland would be chosen. He was on the fringe of England honours. A bit of luck now and he might gain that prized first cap.

When the team was published in the evening newspaper, Billy was on a business trip in London. As expected, Uttley had been chosen as Number 2 jumper in the line. But there in the small print that contained the names of the six replacements, was W. B. Beaumont (Fylde). He could hardly contain his excitement. Liquid celebration was the order of the day and he and his uncle, Joseph, celebrated in true northern style.

Traditionally, players in the England team do not play for their clubs in the week preceding an international. But as Beaumont was a replacement, not a selection, he duly turned out for Fylde against Nuneaton, surviving injury and playing with a new confidence and authority. Afterwards, in the clubhouse, he found himself the subject of a worried conversation between club secretary, Arthur Bell, and England selector, John Elders. Had he broken a cardinal rule by playing? The reality was more serious. Beaumont was one of several players who had been named by the IRA as possible targets should they travel to Dublin. The only person who seemed to take the news lightly was Beaumont himself – it would need an atom bomb to keep him off the bench on the Saturday. As history records, he and his colleagues returned unscathed though the security before they left, and later in Dublin, was unprecedented and intimidating. What history does not record – at least in the record books – was that Beaumont also won his first cap that day thanks to an errant piece of apple pie!

Poor, unfortunate Roger Uttley, whose career was dogged by accident and ill luck, managed to put out his back on the train travelling to London simply because he bent awkwardly to retrieve a pie. Beaumont was with the rest of the squad training at the Stoop Memorial ground near Twickenham when the news was relayed to him by prop Robin Cowling. He couldn't believe it, and it was only when England's chairman of selectors, Alec Lewis, came to his room on the Friday morning before the match to confirm the news that it finally sunk in.

After that, events moved with bewildering speed. They shared their Dublin hotel with the Irish team for security reasons and Billy was horrified to learn that he would be opposing Ireland's living legend, Willie John McBride, in the front of the line-out. It seemed the kind of scenario that had 'one cap wonder' written all over it. Beaumont was twenty-three, a tender age for a lock. McBride was in his thirties and had seen it all and done it all – not many players had taken him on and got the better of it. Furthermore, Willie John was making his first international appearance in Irish colours since leading the Lions on their historic and brilliantly successful safari in South Africa. It was likely to be a baptism of fire.

When kick off-time finally arrived, Billy was both nervous and excited. The England dressing room was awash with telegrams of congratulations for the new cap but he sensibly put them to one side for reading after the game. He wanted to concentrate on one thing only, playing his heart out for England. Sure enough, McBride turned out to be every bit as rugged a customer as Billy had expected. No smiles, no quarter. Off the field he was – and is – the most charming of men, but he had a killer instinct which Beaumont himself would later demonstrate, and for now, his one thought was to get the better of this gangling youngster who stood between him and the ball. He climbed all over Beaumont at the first

11

line-out and it looked as though Billy might truly be out of his depth. But just as the self-doubt began to creep in, England's captain Fran Cotton came over and offered a few well chosen words of advice. Roughly translated, what he said was 'get stuck in', although the message had a stronger ring to it at the time. And that is exactly what Beaumont did. The next ball that came for him to contest, he jumped across and in front of McBride, tapping the ball down for scrum half Jan Webster to collect. It was honours even and, for the first time, Beaumont began to see his opponent in human proportions and began to relax. Ireland won the game 12-9 despite England having held the initiative throughout and actually leading 9-6 with ten minutes to go. It was a sickening disappointment.

3

1976: ENGLAND SLIP OVER THE PRECIPICE

The 1976 season was to prove a low-water mark in English rugby history. A succession of chaotic decisions by the selectors resulted in one badly balanced international team following another, and despite a freak 23-6 win over the touring Australians in January, England reaped the whirlwind.

John Burgess had resigned as coach soon after England returned from down under. Rightly or wrongly, he accepted full responsibility for the mediocre level of performance and the defeats in both test matches. Many critics – and Beaumont is one of them – believed he was wrong to make the supreme sacrifice. That 1975 touring party was one of the weakest England have ever sent abroad and it was almost impossible for a vibrant, lead-from-the-front coach like Burgess to rouse his men. Perhaps coaxing might have stiffened the resolve of some of the players but it could hardly have been expected to sharpen their skills.

Peter Colston of Bristol was the man chosen to succeed. He was a worthy enough candidate with a proven track record. But the suggestion being voiced among players and press was that the close-season surgery had been applied in the wrong place. The coach, after all, is only a limb: the body-corporate is the selection panel, and the chairman its heart. Yet despite the débâcle in Australia the status quo was maintained. Alec Lewis retained the chair and his colleagues supported him. What England needed above all was a good showing in the international championship to silence the critics. But the portents were ominous.

To prepare for the visit of the Wallabies, the selectors decided on a series of three trial matches on successive Saturdays. It was a curious step, a throwback to a system last employed fifty years previously and discarded then on the grounds that full justice could not be done to two candidates for one position from the same region. Barry Bowker, in his definitive book, *England Rugby*, records the following mish-mash employed over the years.

'1874-1909: North v South – sometimes two fixtures a season, with the second before the Calcutta Cup match. (In this series the South won twenty-seven, the North fourteen and three were drawn.) 1910-24: England v North. England v South. England v The Rest. 1925-70: Whites v Colours. Probables v Possibles. England v The Rest. 1971-1974: Two area trials involving South East and Metropolitan, Midlands, South West and South and North, followed by Probables v Possibles and England v The Rest. 1975: England v North and Midlands. England v South and West. England v The Rest.'

Beaumont found himself in the England team for the first trial but it struck him as odd that the North and Midlands should be led by Peter Wheeler of Leicester who seemed a banker to succeed John Pullin as the England hooker. Pullin had been dropped after thirty-seven appearances (thirty-six of them consecutive) the previous season after England's poor showing against Ireland and although he had reverted to captain after Neary's injury in Australia, it seemed obvious that this great servant of English rugby had reached the end of the international road. Beaumont's doubts about the England side were confirmed. Wheeler's men proved far more resolute and the North and Midland's 18-10 victory was a comprehensive spanner thrown into the selectorial works.

There was 'panic in the boardroom'. The England side that took on the South and West at Gloucester the following Saturday showed no less than seven changes. Beaumont's form had held up well, despite being on the losing side, and he survived the axe comfortably. But in the back of his mind was the nagging suspicion that his England career depended on external factors: the whims of the selectors, and the form and preference of another player.

That other player was Roger Uttley of Gosforth, England's most versatile forward but prone to accident and injury in a way that was to blight his career at every level of the game. Uttley was tall, strong and surprisingly fast. He could operate equally successfully as a lock, jumping at the front of the line-out, or as a blindside flanker or Number 8. His preference then was to play at lock but where he would be chosen was anyone's guess.

This time, however, the form book held good – but only just. England won a dull encounter 11-3 but only three of the senior side lost their places for the grand finale, England v The Rest, at Twickenham. Beaumont was not one of them. He retained his place after a rugged, energetic erformance and seemed to be improving with every match. The last hurdle proved to be the easiest. The Rest won precious little ball in the final trial and the England backs made full use of their possession to rattle up 39 points against 21. There was something close to euphoria in the home camp and the selectors quickly agreed to field an unchanged side against Australia in a fortnight's time. So Billy Beaumont was set to win his fourth cap and, as it turned out, get his first taste of victory at international level.

The Wallabies proved to be a pale shadow of the team that had outgunned England twice on the

15

summer tour. The violence, mercifully, had gone from their play, but so, it seemed, had some of the fire and they came to Twickenham with a record that showed four defeats, including internationals against Scotland and Wales.

The England match at headquarters is always the highlight of a Wallaby tour and it seemed that every expatriate Australian in Europe was in London on that cold, sunny afternoon. England won going away although the visitors were lively enough to begin with and indeed, the half-time score of 6-3 to England suggested a close tussle to come. But something in the half time oranges must have fired English ambitions: the pack came out hunting after the break and Australia were buried 23-3. Beaumont impressed me mightily that day, ramrod stiff in the scrum and voracious in the loose. Only the backs performed patchily, three tries being scant pickings from a rich seam of possession.

There was little time for Billy to savour the victory or the manner of his own performance. The international championship was just a fortnight hence and England's first game was against the mighty Welsh at Twickenham. He still couldn't shake off the feeling that the England lock position was his only by the grace of Uttley's injuries and in the days leading up to the game, he trained harder than he had ever done in his life.

'It wasn't an inferiority complex on my part,' he maintains. 'I was just being realistic. There had been so much juggling going on that you never knew what policy the selectors were going to adopt next. I'd be the first to admit that luck – being in the right place at the right time – played an important part in shaping the first half of my career.'

Uttley had not been in contention for the Australian match. A back injury during the England v North and Midlands trial had ruled him out for several weeks and working his way back to peak

16

fitness was a slow and taxing process. Ironically, he was to make his first class comeback on the very morning of the England-Wales pipe opener at Twickenham. And it was to end in disaster.

Traditionally, the morning of an international in the capital sees the London clubs take on their most attractive opponents. A spectator on his way to Twickenham can take in the action at Roehampton or Richmond in mid-morning, have a lively lunch in the crowded pubs near the ground and still be in plenty of time for a 2.15 kick off. It all adds up to a feast of rugby and for the clubs along the route, a welcome boost to finances. Gates can easily be doubled if the opposition is attractive and Uttley's crusaders from the North East, Gosforth, certainly came into that category.

Richmond were their hosts at the Athletic ground and they were soon having a hard time containing their northern visitors. Uttley was in outstanding form, clearly out to prove a point to the selectors by playing in the second row, and jumping with spectacular strength and precision at the front of the line-out. Then tragedy struck. Uttley broke his leg. Only those who were there and saw the look of disbelief mingled with the pain on those craggy features could truly appreciate the dimension of the event. Meanwhile, a few miles to the west, his *bête noire*, Billy Beaumont, was going nervously through his pre-match routine oblivious of the whims of Dame Fortune. It was to be he and not his rival from the other side of the Pennines who would share England's fortunes during the international season. And in the end, it was to prove a highly dubious honour.

Wales came to Twickenham as reigning international champions and had actually strengthened their side by the inclusion at fly half of Phil Bennett. That he should have been missing in the first place was a mystery to English supporters – missing, not

17

just from the side, but excluded from the Welsh squad. He was, at that time, simply the best outside half in the world; the pivot who had helped the Lions destroy South Africa in 1974 and he was still short of his peak.

But England have never held the monopoly on selectorial idiosyncrasies, and the chain of events that saw Bennett nominally reduced from number one fly half to number three behind the competent John Bevan and the promising David Richards, was pure comedy of errors.

Bennett had missed the Welsh victory over Australia due to a foot injury sustained in a match for his club, Llanelli. But having declared himself unfit for international duty, he later answered an emergency call to arms for a crucial club match. He agreed to play only on the strict understanding that he would fetch, carry and pass – but in no circumstances kick the ball. That's how it turned out and Llanelli won the match. But the Welsh selectors were flabbergasted that he had played at all. Black mark to Bennett.

Then, when the final Welsh trial came around, Bennett was a mysterious flu victim, like many a distinguished Welshman before him who abhorred trials in general and Welsh trials in particular. Black mark number two, and under the selectors' totting-up process, it was like a ban from driving. Bennett was left out of the squad and in Wales the headlines screamed their fury and bewilderment.

But once again, it was the selectors who ended up with egg all over their faces. Just before the game Bevan was forced to drop out through illness, and when Richards pulled a hamstring badly enough for him to miss training, Bennett got his licence back. Now the tiny genius from Llanelli would embark on a second career and it was England who were to feel the full weight of his talent.

History records that Wales beat England on the

17th of January, 1976, by 21 points to 9 – their highest winning total at Twickenham for sixty-six years. Yet the statistics blur the positive aspects of England's performance that day. The pack played well – really well. Beaumont had his best game yet in England colours, matching the wily and experienced Geoff Wheel at the front of the line-out and revealing a new dimension to his play by his prominence in the loose.

This sudden 'visibility' surprised many people but it didn't surprise northerners. His all-action game was on display up there every week. What had happened was that Beaumont had finally picked up the pace of international rugby. If you ask any player what they remember most about their debut at international level I guarantee they will answer, 'The speed of the play.' Debutants, especially forwards, find themselves concentrating so hard on the simple mechanics of their job that, often, they don't think themselves into a position to contribute elsewhere. Beaumont had been through that experience but now had the measure of his position and was ready to expand his conception of the game.

England suffered that day for two reasons. Firstly, they were up against the most talented backline in world rugby (*and* they were on song) and secondly, they made elementary defensive mistakes which can be put down to lack of concentration. Beaumont maintains that the difference between English and Welsh sides – as a rule of thumb – is that the Welsh are so used to playing under pressure, day in, day out, that they are always at a pitch of concentration. They can't afford to make simple mistakes, so they purge them from their game. He maintains, too, that Welsh forwards use the ball better and are less hidebound by tactics. In short, they are adaptable.

Bennett, and those Welsh folk heroes, Gareth Edwards and J. P. R. Williams, chose Twickenham as the setting for virtuoso displays. J.P.R. scored twice, once when well covered, but using his strength and determination to break the tackle. Gareth's try was typical of him and typical of England. The home side heeled untidily on their own ball near the line and the Welsh scrum half darted in to snatch up the ball and dive over. England's nine points came from the boot of full-back Alistair Hignell.

With Uttley out for the season, Beaumont was growing in stature with every game. He began to find himself for the first time looking forward to each new challenge. He felt there were many positive aspects about the England performance at Twickenham which could make life difficult for Scotland, their next opponents, in the Calcutta Cup match at Murrayfield. He wasn't alone. The selectors, too, seemed well satisfied and gave the side a rare vote of confidence. It seemed to most observers that England had found a pack at least the equal of anything in the other countries, and if they could only tighten up their back play – who knows?

Before the match, both teams were presented to Her Majesty the Queen and Prince Philip. It was to be Billy's first (but not the last) meeting with the Sovereign and he recalls it still as one of the highlights of his career. He remembers how inspired he felt afterwards and how the same feeling seemed to affect the rest of the England players. They began the game as if they had a train to catch.

4

1976: WHITEWASH!

Many of the 70,000 crowd that packed Murrayfield were still shuffling into their seats when England's flying winger, Ken Plummer, plunged over in the corner for what looked like a sensational try. Sadly for the English, play was called back when a touch judge signalled that Plummer had clipped a foot into touch trying to evade Andy Irvine's despairing tackle. But try or not, it was just the kind of positive start the visitors needed and it was no surprise at all when they did make one count in the sixth minute.

Andy Maxwell, the burly Headingley centre, was strong enough to crash through the Scots' defence after fly half Alan Old had collected a loose ball in the midfield, and with Hignell slotting an accurate conversion, England were 6-0 ahead. The score gave the visitors real momentum and the forwards began to push their opponents back significantly in the set scrums. With Andy Ripley, Mark Keyworth, Tony Neary, Bob Wilkinson and Beaumont behind those craggy front row customers, Mike Burton and Fran Cotton, it was no wonder the Scots had such a torrid time. But as is so often the case in international sport, the margins of superiority are made suddenly irrelevant by one touch of genius or inspiration from the beleaguered camp.

So it was this time. David Shedden, the West of Scotland winger, caught an attacking kick ahead and when he was held up, launched the ball inside to Mike Biggar. The London Scottish flanker linked with Sandy Carmichael, who handed on to the giant Alan

21

Tomes, and finally, scrum half Alan Lawson came bursting through to cap a sparkling movement with a brilliant try.

This potential body blow was nullified by some accurate place kicking by Old who put over two penalties to one by Irvine and thus kept England's nose in front, 12-9, at the interval. It was in the cruelly disappointing second half that the limitations of the selectors' vision at last became apparent.

The pack was solid and admirable; the three-quarters speedy and sound. But the choice of the strong but erratic Mike Lampkowski at scrum half quickly proved eccentric. England had been looking for a home-grown version of Gareth Edwards – a scrum half big enough and bullish enough to take on a wall of defenders and prevail. They were looking, too, for someone who could capitalise on quick possession near the opposing line and dart in for opportunist tries. Edwards had demonstrated that he had no peer as a poacher at Twickenham. But equally, he had the fastest, longest and most accurate pass in world rugby harnessed by a footballing brain that could react a vital split second before his colleagues.

The writing had been on the wall in the game against Australia where he had persisted in running into blind alleys, soaking up punishment like a heavyweight boxer in an effort to suck in the opposition. It was brave, red-blooded stuff, but against a side like the Wallabies it had proved merely an irritation. There had been too much possession going England's way for Lampkowski's forays to prove profligate. Even the Welsh match had proved nothing. Edwards (his opponent) had dominated better scrum halves than the England man so judgement was difficult and easily deferred. But in the seething blue cauldron of Murrayfield with a slender lead and a pack rampant and eager, it was Lampkowski's signal duty to get his backline moving

22

at each and every opportunity, especially as Alan Old was kicking so well he could always orchestrate play.

Beaumont remembers with a sense of awe and wonder watching Lampkowski squander the best and cleanest possession of the game with a series of suicidal breaks from the base of the scrum which, without exception, ended with him being flattened. With Old and his colleagues starving outside him, their confidence began to ebb away. Perhaps England's captain, Tony Neary, should have grasped the nettle and called the play, but on this occasion his instructions were either ignored, or else not forthcoming, and the general malaise began to overtake the whole team.

Scotland defended stoutly, roared on by a partisan crowd, and whenever a sniff of a chance came their way, they were on to it like hungry wolves. Irvine had levelled the scores with a penalty for a careless England infringement and when Old, for once, was hesitant with a defensive clearing kick, David Leslie, the West of Scotland flanker, charged the ball down, collected the bounce and ran through twenty-five yards to score.

England might have come back but Scotland would not let them. Their forwards became inspired and the pressure mounted on the England line as the precious minutes ticked inexorably away. Finally, Lawson dummied his way into an inviting gap to score his second try. Irvine was on target with the conversion and the final whistle sounded soon after.

The 22-12 scoreline suggests comfortable superiority for the Scots, but it need not have been so. It was one of the most depressing defeats in Beaumont's short international career and he, like his colleagues, anticipated wholesale changes for the next match against the Irish.

To add to the general mood of gloom and doom caused by the Calcutta Cup result there was the injury to England's one world class threequarter, David

Duckham. The blond Coventry player had been troubled by a series of niggling hamstring injuries for a couple of seasons. In 1975 he had looked unfit and played accordingly and serious questions were now being asked about his commitment and his worth. Against Australia he had made the most of a little and scored a neat try to suggest that he might be on his way back. Against Wales, he rarely saw the ball, but on the two occasions that he did, the suspect hamstring had held up.

Before facing Scotland, however, Duckham decided that he should prove to himself and his team mates that his fitness was one hundred per cent. It was typical of him that he should most fear letting down his colleagues so a strenuous pre-match session with the England doctor, Dr Leo Walkden, was arranged. Dr Walkden stretched and twisted and contorted every suspect muscle and Duckham felt not a twinge. He was duly pronounced fit and he took to the field with a new confidence and his appetite for the game fully restored.

The match was just ten minutes old when Lampkowski made a surprise break down the left and found Duckham at his right shoulder up in support. The scrum half released the ball to the winger in full stride and Duckham took it on the burst. The shock of what happened next is lodged in his mind like shrapnel.

'Four strides later what felt like a rifle shot racked the back of my leg with agonising pain. Approximately one second later a Sherman tank appeared out of nowhere in the form of Scottish left wing, David Shedden, who tackled me up into the tenth row of the stand. Even at that moment I knew I would not take the field again that season. I needed assistance to get to my feet and it must have seemed to many of the onlookers that it was David Shedden's comprehensive tackle which caused my departure from the field. I was numb with disappointment and disbelief.'

In the end, the selectors made only one voluntary change for the next game, Gary Adey coming in for the giant Andy Ripley at Number 8. With Duckham ruled out a new wing was needed and Liverpool's Mike Slemen got the vote to win his first cap. Thus was another link forged in the chain that would lead to England's Grand Slam in 1980.

The Irish match was expected to be tough because all matches against Ireland are that. But at least it would be at Twickenham, where the crowd was less likely to lift the Greens to the fever pitch customary at Landsdowne Road, Dublin. On the other hand, English supporters tend to demand a running game from their side at headquarters: they have little patience with grinding, remorseless forward battles and like to see the backs brought into the play at every opportunity. England's strength, however precarious, in that traumatic 1976 season was up front and Beaumont saw their best chance of victory lay in sucking the tearaway Irish back row into maul and ruck, maul and ruck until their speed to the breakdown was nullified and their appetite diminished. It didn't work out that way.

Lampkowski, stung no doubt by criticism of his role in the Scottish débâcle, seemed inclined to give whatever expression he could to the England threequarters by spinning the ball out. Too often it was 'bad' ball and attacker and defender would appear at the same moment with predictable results. England simply couldn't make progress and the Irish were ready to feed on every mistake.

In Barry McGann, Ireland had a fly half who was in every sense a footballer. He was the epitome of calm when Irish exuberance caused them to give away three early penalties, which Alan Old duly converted. But McGann was content to wait, accepting the two penalty chances that came his way and dropping the sweetest of goals to cap Tom Grace's opportunist try. The Greens won 13-12 and England's season of hope was in tatters.

Lampkowski didn't survive the defeat. He was axed for the next game, against France in Paris, and later was to switch codes to Rugby League where his particular style coupled with strength and aggression was to prove much better suited. So at the end of the day England were staring at a potential whitewash in the championship, something that had only happened once before in their history, in 1972 – but significantly, in the same decade. They might have salvaged something from the wreckage if they hadn't had the misfortune to come upon perhaps the finest French side that country has ever produced. The spring sunshine was warm, the turf inviting and England were annihilated. The score, 30-9, flattered them because on that day, fifty or even sixty points were well within the Frenchmen's grasp.

Steve Smith, whom Beaumont felt should have played scrum half for England throughout the campaign, finally got the selectors' nod. Sadly for the young man eager to impress, it was fully twenty minutes before he even got a touch of the ball so dominant was the French pack. Making his debut that afternoon for France was one Jean Pierre Rives whose impact was so astounding that R.F.U. president, Dickie Jeeps, in his address at the banquet after the game, singled him out for special mention – an honour almost without precedent on such occasions.

This was such a good French side that it would be churlish to criticise the selectors for failing to choose an England team capable of holding them. But criticised they must be for an incident before the match which in its bungling and insensitivity might stand as a monument to all that was wrong with English rugby in the early seventies.

To partner the recalled Steve Smith, the selectors had chosen the Moseley stand-off Martin Cooper. Alan Old was dropped, but designated to sit on the replacements' bench. It was thus logical to assume that if Cooper dropped out before the game or was injured during it, then the Yorkshireman would take over at fly half. Not so. There had been a question mark over Cooper's fitness — he'd been injured in a club game — and on the Thursday before the game in Paris, he was put through a rigorous fitness test. Billy recalls wryly that if he had been fit before the test there was no prospect of him being fit after it. It lasted a full hour and was punishing from start to finish. Old sums up what followed next this way:

'After the session, Cooper was told he wouldn't be playing fly half, and neither would I. Instead, the selectors told us that newcomer Chris Williams would be winning his first cap. I wasn't the only member of the team who wasn't very pleased with the situation. It was another fine example of man-management.'

Old was undoubtedly one of the best — and unluckiest — players in international rugby. He had made his debut in 1972 and been chosen for the British Lions party to tour South Africa. His form was so outstanding during the early part of that tour (a record thirty-seven points in one match) that his selection for the test fly half spot opposite Gareth Edwards seemed to many a foregone conclusion. But then came a vicious late tackle in one of the provincial games that not only put him out of the test reckoning but into hospital with a broken arm. Phil Bennett of Wales played instead and the rest is history.

Old is philosophical about his up-and-down international career but what he says goes a long way to explaining just why England got it so wrong in the early years of the seventies. 'I think the selectors played hunches,' he says, 'tending towards players who might become good in a few years' time. But they didn't, or rather, weren't given the chance to. What is vital in international rugby is experience, but these were the very players who were neglected. Nigel

27

Horton was in and out of the England team. Of the seven Englishmen on the 1974 Lions tour only Fran Cotton, Mike Burton and Roger Uttley were used to any extent by England when they returned.

'The great tragedy for me at this time was Jan Webster of Moseley. He put in two tremendous games in the away wins over South Africa and New Zealand. That performance of his against the All Blacks is the finest I have ever seen at international level. But for England's next game – against Australia at Twickenham – Steve Smith's longer pass got him the place. Again they were playing a hunch instead of sticking to the best players available. Players at international level have got to have confidence in the players around them, something you can't have in players who haven't proved themselves.'

One player who had proved himself and emerged from the carnage of a wooden spoon international season with reputation enhanced was William Blackledge Beaumont. No finger of accusation could be pointed in his direction. But there were casualties galore elsewhere.

Chris Williams, whose selection had sparked off such controversy, had played well with limited opportunities in Paris. His reward? He never played for England again. Joining him on the international scrapheap would be John Pullin, Andy Ripley's premature replacement at Number 8, Gary Adey, Billy Beaumont's second row partner, Bob Wilkinson, full back Peter Butler, wing Ken Plummer, and centres Andy Maxwell and David Cooke. But the selectors did not survive unscathed either. Alec Lewis gave way as chairman to Sandy Sanders, a wise and affable man, and on to the committee for the first time came three players who had had first-hand experience of playing rugby in the seventies and were thus more attuned to the players' needs – Budge Rogers, Mike Weston and Derek Morgan.

28

The lessons of 1976 were certainly not lost on Billy Beaumont. Once he became truly established – and there were to be stutters on the way – he at once put into practice much of what he had learned in that bitter winter. Communication with players, with committee-men, with press, was to be a hallmark of his later captaincy. There would be no secrets, no decisions behind closed doors. Each player would be made to feel immediately part of the team and encouraged to express himself and play to his strengths.

But for now, there was only a bleak set of statistics for him to reflect upon. Another wooden spoon and England's second whitewash in four years. In the last two years, no less than forty-six men had worn the white shirt of England in international matches with five more going to Australia and remaining uncapped. It is a turnover that boggles the mind.

No wonder then that England rugby historian Barry Bowker ruefully noted at the end of his book, 'By 1976, England's rugby had reached a very low ebb.'

5

1977: DAWNING AMBITION

A British Lions test series in New Zealand is the
ultimate rugby contest and just to be one of the
touring party represents a pinnacle in any career.
Such an accolade seemed a million light years away
from Billy Beaumont as he threw himself into the
relentless grind of pre-season training at the end of
the long, hot summer of 1976.

It had been a crazy four months. The sun blazed
remorselessly from a blue sky throughout May, June
and July, squeezing every last drop of moisture from
the parched land. The temperature was rarely out of
the eighties and for much of the time, ninety degrees
was the norm. By the middle of August, Britain was
tinder dry and forest fires and dried-up reservoirs had
become so commonplace they were no longer front
page news.

Normally, the wind on the Fylde coast is sharp and
bracing, but in 1976 it was suffocating. The pitch at
Fylde rugby club was a scorched brown handkerchief
and underfoot, the ground was as unyielding as
concrete. Other clubs suffered more. Those where the
grass seed hadn't taken or had blown away on the
breeze simply broke up in a zig zag of deep, wide
fissures. Water was rationed; groundsmen gave up in
despair.

But throughout those stifling, relentless days,
Beaumont kept his eye fixed on the calendar. The
Lions were to leave England the following May. They
would be flying in to the soft autumn rains of
Christchurch and Dunedin, paddling through green

grass that brushed the ankles and running on pitches that took a stud right up to the leather soles of their boots.

It was a powerful image, as clear as the crisp New Zealand air, and he fuelled his vision with punishing training sessions in the furnace that was Britain. When September arrived, sluggish and reluctant to usher in the new season, he was fitter than he had ever been in his life. The form book of the previous season was thrown out of the window as freak playing conditions produced freak results, but Fylde started well and Beaumont was quick to catch the eye of the Lancashire selectors.

The County showed murderous form, decimating their opponents and sweeping to the top of the Northern Group table. Argentina were the visitors to Britain that year, a country not yet acknowledged as a true force in international rugby, but full of flair and running. So full of running, in fact, that they came within an ace of toppling the mighty Welsh at the Arms Park, and yet, when they met the North and Midlands at Leicester, they were crushed 24-9. Beaumont had a big hand in the victory and so consistent was his play that it seemed a foregone conclusion that he would be named as one of the Whites (the senior side) when the sides for the final England trial at Twickenham were announced.

But once again, the selectors proved myopic and eccentric. He made the trial all right, but found himself consigned to the Rest alongside such luminaries as Andy Ripley, Steve Smith and Dusty Hare. It was a bitter disappointment but by now he had become resigned to the vagaries of committee decisions and instead, he and his colleagues devoted themselves to plotting the tactical downfall of the opposition. In his entertaining autobiography, *Thanks to Rugby*, Billy describes just how the Whites were scuppered:

31

'On the Friday night, (the trial was on New Year's Day) we plotted our line-out tactics. I was to be stationed at the front, Barry Ayres in the middle and Ripley was given a roaming role which worked to perfection. He enjoyed this sort of brief and with the rest of us winning occasional ball and acting as ideal decoys for Ripley we dominated the line-out and were level 3-all at half time. During the interval the selectors made two changes, but they remained blind, oblivious or ignorant to the role Ripley was playing so successfully. Ayres and myself were promoted to the England team in place of Bob Wilkinson and Roger Powell and we ran out comfortable winners in the second half by twenty points to three.'

Scotland, who had 'stolen' the Calcutta Cup at Murrayfield the previous season, were to be England's opponents in the opening match of the new campaign, and it was clear from the England selection that a game plan had been devised, and personnel had been chosen who could follow that plan to the letter. Some talented players were left on the sidelines but Billy conceded that the thinking had a positive edge to it and he found himself looking forward to the game with mounting excitement.

In essence, England had conceded that Scotland owned the more skilful backs and set out to field a pack of forwards that would deny them the ball. The game would be kept as tight as possible. To counter any attacking moves by the Scots, England had two of the best defensive centres in the game, the tenacious Barry Corless and the rugged, intimidating Charles Kent. The plan worked to perfection.

Scotland saw so little of the ball that heads began to drop and the defensive cover evaporate. England capitalised by running in four superb tries and though the final score of 26-6 appears to be a thrashing, it actually flattered the Scots. Veteran Twickenham-watchers sensed a new mood in the air. The team was young and enthusiastic and its power base, the pack, was powerful indeed. Perhaps the dog days were finally over.

In Dublin, England repeated the pattern of play that had hammered the Scots. Conditions favoured their approach. The pitch was slimy, the rain relentless and only a fool or a juggler would relish handling in such conditions. So Beaumont and his colleagues simply pushed and grappled and slithered and relied on the boot of fly half Martin Cooper to keep the Irish pinned back in their own half. If ever Beaumont was called upon to prove his fitness it was now, and this match was an eloquent testimonial to those punishing summer training runs. The one disappointment as the minutes ticked away was England's inability to fashion a score out of their surfeit of possession. But the deadlock was finally broken when full back Alistair Hignell sent in a perfect diagonal kick which Cooper chased, gathered and carried over the Irish line. One try was enough. There was no further scoring.

There was euphoria in the England camp. Two consecutive wins – and worthy wins at that – had taken them to joint leadership of the international table with an impressive points aggregate of thirty for and only six against. Even the mighty Welsh must respect that, surely? But the French were next and those who had played in Paris when Rives and Bastiat and Skrela had run and handled like basketball players were under no illusions about what awaited them. The main point in England's favour was that the match would be at Twickenham, very much a bogey ground for the French.

Actually, Twickenham was a bogey ground for most teams, with the exception of the Welsh. Many a brilliant individual had frozen in that amphitheatre. But it wasn't just the atmosphere. Twickenham was an architectural freak, producing swirling winds

33

above the stands and dead air below. To kick well, a full back had to be lucky or knowledgeable, like Bob Hiller, who used to play at Twickenham perhaps twenty times a season in either England or Harlequins colours. The former England captain knew every nook and cranny, every mood and shift of wind. He had kept his country afloat during the bleak years from 1968 to 1972 when they had better results than the teams ever merited.

But France had no Hiller and neither, on that day, did England. Alistair Hignell was the designated place kicker and he had a miserable afternoon. Of six kickable penalties, he managed to land just one. And England, despite turning in yet another surging forward performance and containing the dangerous French back row, came away on the wrong end of a 4-3 scoreline after a dubious try by Sangali. The bubble had burst. You need luck as well as skill to win international rugby matches and it seemed that for the present, England's had run out.

The prospect of tackling the Welsh in the final match at the Arms Park filled many of the players with dread – but Beaumont was not one of them. Still his form had held up and now there were two thoughts uppermost in his mind as he contemplated the wall of sound that would greet him in Cardiff. First, despite the French setback, England were still in with a chance of the Triple Crown. They only had to beat Wales. Only! The second thought concerned the Lions tour which had hardly been out of his mind all winter and was now within touching distance if he could play out of his skin in Cardiff.

Such is the stuff of dreams. But, realistically, he knew he'd had a good season – the best of his life. Against Argentina for the North and Midlands he had been superb. He also won plaudits from the press for his play against Scotland and France. Ireland had proved his stamina. Lancashire – who had won the County Championship – had given him a taste for victory. Above all, he had proved he was no second row donkey, no 'reserve' jumper whose sole asset was an ability to push. Instead, he had developed into a prolific and effective forward in the loose; deceptively quick and mighty hard to knock over.

With the season almost over, the newspapers were full of speculation on the possible Lions party. After the victories in New Zealand in 1971 and South Africa in 1974, British rugby was regarded as the strongest in the world. It seemed to many you only had to dip a hand into the bran tub to pull out a top class centre or prop or scrum half. And it was true there were some talented players about. But a realistic pundit would have observed that players like Gareth Edwards, J. P. R. Williams, Gerald Davies, Fergus Slattery and a few others were the cream of the crop. If they could not or would not tour, what then?

Beaumont was realistic enough to pose such questions. As an insider, 'on the circuit', as it were, he was aware of persistent rumours concerning the stars. Not everyone relished a four-month tour in one of the remotest countries on earth. Some, who were in the evening, or at least, late afternoon of their careers were already finding the constant pressure a strain. But most of the rumours concerned the backs, the 'stars of the show'. The forwards were a different matter. There would be few refusals in the front row union or the engine room of the scrum. So the question for Beaumont was, 'how many do I have to beat to get on that plane?' He listed the possibilities.

The best lock in Britain was undoubtedly Gordon Brown, one of the heroes of South Africa in 1974 and by common consent, a big match player. But Brown was also a maverick, not beloved of all rugby authorities and indeed, an absentee throughout the 1977 international season due to suspension. Would his form or his appetite be sharp enough for New Zealand? Beaumont conceded it probably would, knowing Brown. He would see it as the greatest challenge and as he was the best, he ought to be picked, suspension or no suspension. So pencil him in.

The next candidate was Nigel Horton of England. Beaumont's second row partner had played as well as Beaumont that year and being the main jumper in the side, operating in the middle of the line-out, he had the advantage of being more visible. Pencil him in too. Brown was good enough to play front or middle so it was probable, reasoned Beaumont, the selectors would want another out and out jumper in the final quartet. That narrowed it down to Moss Keane of Ireland and Allan Martin of Wales. Martin was like a stag. He could take off with lead weights tied to his ankles and in the mud of New Zealand, that could give him a crucial edge.

That left one spot and this time it would have to be an out and out front of the line-out specialist. Who was there? There was Geoff Wheel of Wales. And there was . . . well, himself. No point in being over-modest about it, and as the Welshman had probably done his sums and reached the same conclusions it looked like they could be in for a bit of a ding dong battle down in Cardiff. Beaumont didn't confide his ambitions to either friends or colleagues, but privately, he promised himself he would beat his opponent out of sight and make that summer dream of 1976 a winter reality.

England were given some sort of chance against Wales. It was acknowledged, even in the valleys, that they had been moral victors over the French, and as France had beaten Wales and now looked unstoppable in their bid for the Grand Slam, England, ergo, should beat Wales. Some hope. The Welshmen were not about to pass up a Triple Crown, especially not to the English. Their pack sizzled that day; Allan Martin won so much line-out ball it was embarrassing, and Gareth Edwards spent the afternoon lobbing the ball to any Welsh back who fancied a run.

36

Curiously, for all their superiority front and back, Wales only managed two tries, one by J. P. R. Williams – his fifth against England – the other by Gareth himself – a record breaking nineteen in Welsh colours. The final score was 14-9, which suggests near parity, but in fact stands as a tribute to Hignell the full back who made amends for his wretched time against France by keeping England vaguely in the hunt with three penalties.

But outside of the context of the game, there were larger battles being fought. Allan Martin outjumped Horton and removed all doubts about his fitness to be part of the touring Lions and Derek Quinnell eclipsed England's captain Roger Uttley at Number 8. Both were Lions certainties but Uttley was a candidate for the captaincy. What were his chances now?

And saddest of all, Beaumont lost his private duel with Wheel. The Englishman was brave, too brave perhaps with the Welshmen in full cry. All too often his determination and adventure led him into blind alleys from which the only escape was underground. One classic photograph that remains of the match appeared in *Rugby World* and shows Billy halted by Burgess' tackle looking round for a colleague to pass to. But the sight that greets him is a forest of red shirts, Price, Cobner and Martin to the fore with Wheel close behind.

As he wiped the mud of battle from his boots and drank hot, sweet tea in the steam-filled dressing room after the game, Beaumont closed his eyes and began doing some more mental arithmetic. Wheel plus Brown, Brown plus Martin, Horton and Martin . . . and so on. But whichever way he figured it, there was no place for W. B. Beaumont. He sighed. It had been a nice dream but it looked like it was finally over.

6

1977: WHEEL OF FORTUNE

Meanwhile, the international season had ended on a
high note for Wales and their popular captain, Phil
Bennett. His form had been consistently brilliant and
he was an overwhelming choice as Player of the Year
in the prestigious annual *Rugby World* poll. There
was joy in the principality too over the selection of
John Dawes to coach the Lions in New Zealand and
given the success of Welsh sides coached by Dawes it
seemed inevitable that where there might be any
doubt, a Welsh player would get the nod.

And so it proved. Bennett was named captain and
no less than seventeen Welshmen were named in the
thirty strong touring party – including Geoff Wheel.
Beaumont was resigned by now to his fate and he
began to turn his attention instead to a pressing
domestic issue. He had been married in February to
Hilary and the honeymoon had been postponed until
all his rugby commitments were out of the way. Now
he began to make plans.

But Dame Fortune hadn't finished with him yet.
Before the Lions flew out, Wheel was withdrawn
from the party. It was a shock. A routine medical
check had detected a heart irregularity which caused
his doctors concern. A second opinion was
inconclusive but the Lions management felt the risk
of taking him was too great and he was asked to stand
down. Suddenly, the fourth place was up for grabs
again. Billy could hardly contain himself waiting for
the name of the replacement to be announced. He
describes the moment vividly:

'I was driving down the motorway and I heard on the car radio that Wheel's replacement had just been announced. At this moment my heartbeat was so strong it was nearly going through the windscreen, but when I heard the reporter read out the name of Moss Keane I was shattered. It meant the selectors had decided to set off without a recognised front jumper. That could only mean they thought there was no one good enough in the British Isles and I took that as a little bit of an affront. At least I knew exactly where I stood in the estimation of the selectors and I promptly went out and booked a fortnight's honeymoon in Minorca.'

A few days later he received a letter from the four home unions' tour committee confirming he had been chosen as a reserve and requesting him to remain on standby throughout the summer. Billy was pleased but not sufficiently impressed enough to cancel his holiday arrangements. It was to prove an expensive mistake.

The thirty-three players that finally left Heathrow on May 10 were not quite the *crème de la crème* of British rugby. As the whispers had suggested, there were some distinguished absentees. Gareth Edwards, lynch pin of the successful tour of South Africa in 1974, had declared himself unavailable. It was a bitter blow made all the more frustrating by the knowledge that both his employer and his wife Maureen had given their blessing. The choice was entirely his, but the truth was that he felt almost burned out by the pressures of the game. He admits that he was even considering retirement altogether. 'Besides,' he adds candidly, 'I had done it all before. I didn't see what else I had to prove.'

Hard on the heels of Gareth's announcement came a crop of other distinguished 'defectors'. Gerald Davies, the magician of the side step, said he couldn't tour. J. P. R. Williams couldn't afford to leave his medical studies at a critical juncture and he too had been eliminated. Fergus Slattery, the tearaway Irish flanker, also declined the four-month long commitment.

The final blow for the selectors came when Roger Uttley, who had captained England so successfully in their mini revival, lost a desperate battle to recover from a back injury (later diagnosed as a prolapsed disc, and therefore serious). Having lost the captaincy vote on the strength of Wales' display at Cardiff, the genial Gosforth man had now to accept the bitterest blow of all in a career plagued with ill fortune.

The dispute over whether Uttley or Beaumont was the best front of the line jumper in England had been settled once and for all by the England selectors. They had moved the Gosforth man to the back row where he could add height and mobility as well as utilising his great strength. The move had worked as far as it went, but inexplicably, the selectors had then sacrificed the speed of Tony Neary in favour of the grafting of Mike Rafter.

Billy Beaumont was far from alone in questioning the composition of the final tour party. It was loaded heavily with Welshmen, all talented but many woefully inexperienced at international level, let alone touring. No place had been found for the outstanding Scottish centre Jim Renwick. There was no crash tackling specialist in the Ray Gravell mould. The second row was a quartet of middle of the line specialists. And at scrum half, Brynmor Williams and Doug Morgan of Scotland had been chosen to link the forwards and the backs via the giant talent of the little man from Llanelli, Phil Bennett. The point in their case was that as they were so dissimilar in style the test place would clearly be reserved for the one who best suited the Lions' tactical plan. But, if the plan should be changed and the 'wrong' scrum half get injured, what then? There were many ifs, not all legitimate but they underscored the growing

40

nervousness in the rugby press about the Lions' chances.

Most approved the choice of Williams, uncapped for so long and seemingly Gareth Edwards' permanent understudy. But you don't replace a Gareth overnight. In fact, you don't replace him at all by opting for a player with a short, if worthy pass. Bennett has always maintained that Edwards' accuracy and length had been the crucial factor in South Africa. Leaving aside his other attributes of exceptional strength, tactical cunning and indomitable will, it was that precious half-second he gave his outside half to decide on one, two or sometimes three different options that kept the Lions one step ahead throughout that tour. Beaumont admits that had he been a selector, he would have found a place for England's Steve Smith, a player whose talent he had long admired but at that time out of favour with the England selectors. Smith it was who finally succeeded Beaumont as England captain in 1982.

The most striking feature of the whole party was the emphasis on utility. Gareth Evans of Newport was a play anywhere back although nominally chosen for the wing; Bruce Hay of Scotland was the reserve full back who played much of his best rugby on the wing; Moss Keane was a middle line jumper who played at the front; Fran Cotton was equally effective as a loose head or tight head prop. And finally, there was Mike Gibson, the Irish genius who had been a hero with the 1971 Lions but now, at thirty-four, was in the twilight of a great career. He was chosen to cover as fly half, centre and wing, but in the event he was never used (in the tests) as either. All in all there was a lack of experience and a lack of specialists. The full tour party was:

POSITION	CLUB AND COUNTRY	AGE	HEIGHT	WEIGHT
Full backs:				
Andy Irvine	Heriot's FP and Scotland	25	5.10	12.8
Bruce Hay	Boroughmuir and Scotland	27	5.10	13.5
Wingers:				
Peter Squires	Harrogate and England	25	5.9	11.9
John J. Williams	Llanelli and Wales	29	5.9	11.7
Elgan Rees	Neath (uncapped)	23	5.8	12.7
Gareth Evans	Newport and Wales	23	5.11	13.11
Centres:				
Steve Fenwick	Bridgend and Wales	25	5.10	13.2
David Burcher	Newport and Wales	25	5.10	13.5
Mike Gibson	Ulster and Ireland	34	5.10	12.7
Ian McGeechan	Headingly and Scotland	30	5.9	11.3
Fly-halves:				
Phil Bennett (capt.)	Llanelli and Wales	28	5.7	11.4
John Bevan	Aberavon and Wales	29	5.8	12.8
Scrum-halves:				
Douglas Morgan	Stewarts-Melville and Scotland	30	5.9	11.10
Brynmor Williams	Cardiff (uncapped)	25	5.9	12.7
Flankers:				
Trevor Evans	Swansea and Wales	29	6.1	14.4
Terry Cobner	Pontypool and Wales	30	6.0	14.4
Jeff Squire	Newport and Wales	25	6.3	15.7
Number 8:				
Willie Duggan	Blackrock College and Ireland	27	6.3	15.12
Derek Quinnell	Llanelli and Wales	28	6.3	16.7
Locks:				
Gordon Brown	West of Scotland and Scotland	29	6.5	16.12
Allan Martin	Aberavon and Wales	28	6.5	16.8
Nigel Horton	Moseley and England	29	6.5	16.8
Moss Keane	Landsdowne and Ireland	28	6.4	16.13

POSITION	CLUB AND COUNTRY	AGE	HEIGHT	WEIGHT
Props:				
Phil Orr	Old Wesley and Ireland	26	5.11	15.7
Clive Williams	Aberavon and Wales	28	6.0	15.8
Graham Price	Pontypool and Wales	25	6.0	15.4
Fran Cotton	Sale and England	29	6.2	16.7
Hookers:				
Bobby Windsor	Pontypool and Wales	28	5.9	14.9
Peter Wheeler	Leicester and England	28	5.11	14.0

It might have been argued that the management was being prudent in covering most options. After all, four months is a long time and injuries are inevitable. But many at the time argued the case for a Saturday side of specialists, clearly established in the selectors' minds before the off with the balance being chosen because of their similarity and singularity. But there never was such a side. The Lions party was a melting pot and it was to prove two long months into the tour before a consensus emerged.

Finally, the management itself. There were no quibbles over the choice of John Dawes as assistant manager/coach. He had been the inspiration behind Wales and the 1971 Lions as a player and as a captain, and his golden touch had continued with the Welsh team as its coach. His manager, George 'Dod' Burrell of Scotland, was a gentle, amiable man, well versed in the social and diplomatic arts – a crucial qualification for any tour. But for some strange reason, the chemical mix was to prove volatile: Dawes would become over protective of his players, domineering and dogmatic to the point of stubbornness. Burrell would quite simply be overtaken by events, become reclusive as the war of words off the field grew in intensity until it finally commanded more headlines than the reporting of the games.

But all that was in the future, and in any case, in the early summer of 1977 it was a future that seemed to preclude William Beaumont, esquire. His only connection with the great expedition would be via the crackles of a short wave radio or through the match reports in the daily press. And at first, all those reports were encouraging.

The first game was against Wairarapa Bush at Masterton in the middle of May and the Lions got off to a flyer. They put forty-one points on the board, most of them in the second half, but significantly, it was the Wesh contingent who had a field day. The winger, J. J. Williams, ran in three splendid tries. Pontypool's Terry Cobner – later to be so influential on the coaching side – scored twice, as did centre David Burcher, while captain Phil Bennett kicked a penalty goal and three conversions. England winger Peter Squires prevented Wales from achieving a clean sweep with a try of his own but the initial impression of the victory was devastating. Coach John Dawes wore a smile as wide as the Bristol Channel.

The next match was harder, in Napier against the rugged Hawkes Bay. This time the Lions were less prolific (13-3 and only one try, from full back Andy Irvine) but still well in command. Poverty Bay fell 25-6; then Taranaki, 21-13, captained by the bright new star, Graham Mourie; Colin Meads-coached King Country went down 60-9; Manawatu lost 18-12 . . . and so it went on as the Lions appeared to gather momentum.

Back in Britain the early results received rapturous attention in the newspapers. 1977 was Silver Jubilee Year and any excuse for flag waving was seized on hungrily in Fleet Street. Andy Irvine, who played in six of the first seven games and scored five tries against King Country, garnered most of the headlines. But the small print also recorded worrying injuries to Elgan Rees, Doug Morgan and Derek Quinnell while the background stories told of the almost constant rain.

Winning is sport's universal panacea but the truth is the Lions were struggling to find their best form on the heavy grounds and the pace of events both on and off the pitch was already exacting a heavy toll. In reporting to its readers under the bright headline, 'Lions Roar', *Rugby World* was quick to strike a note of caution:

'The performances of the players generally will have made John Dawes quietly optimistic. The Lions are not yet in top gear, though winning. But it still looks as if this is one tour when Lions substitutes, both in New Zealand and here at home will be kept on their toes.'

As those prophetic words were being written, Billy Beaumont was far away from it all, camping in the Lake District with Hilary and a group of friends. It was the Spring Bank Holiday and most of the country was enjoying the warm sunshine and preparing for the rounds of street parties that would distinguish the Queen's Silver Jubilee celebrations. And it was on that very Bank Holiday that rugby's forgotten man got the call to arms. The fact that he received it at all is something of a miracle; an event he remembers with singular clarity:

'When we got back I decided to go into the office to catch up on some paperwork before it re-opened on Wednesday morning. The phone rang in the warehouse and I went across to answer it, assuming it must be a wrong number. It wasn't. The caller was England's representative on the Lions' selection committee, Malcolm Phillips. What he said in effect was, "Nigel Horton has broken his thumb and is out of the tour. The management want you to replace him. Can you fly out immediately?" '

Billy was stunned. Thrilling though the moment obviously was, doubts quickly began to crowd in. Beaumont had sudden visions of two months of frustration slogging away in the Wednesday side – the

Dirt Trackers as they were called by the players – with little or no prospect of making the test team. The injury to Horton had occurred during a bruising battle with Otago which the Lions were fortunate to survive 12-7. At that time, the giant English lock was looking a banker for the first test and it seemed certain his partner would be the big occasion man, Gordon Brown of Scotland. The odds now were that Brown would move into the middle with Moss Keane jumping at the front. Allan Martin could then understudy the middle position. But whichever way you carved it, it seemed to leave Billy holding the short straw.

He discussed his worries with Hilary – remember, there was still that honeymoon booked for July – and she was adamant that he should go and prove to himself, if no one else, just who was the best lock forward in the British Isles. It was the kind of unequivocal response he had hoped for, not that there was ever any real likelihood of him declining the invitation. And as it happened there were factors in his favour that he neither knew about nor could anticipate.

By common reckoning, the Lions were now wobbling. The smooth upward curve of progress had hit a nasty air pocket in Otago, and there was worse to come. Phil Bennett recalls his misgivings at this early stage of the tour in his eye-opening book, *Everywhere for Wales*.

'We were none too impressive in the first quartet of matches. Sometimes we received the occasional nod of approval from former All Blacks and critics, but there was a general lack of conviction about our play. I had an uneasy feeling we were conning ourselves . . . there was an ingredient missing.'

Beaumont's arrival would coincide with the

humiliating 21-9 defeat at the hands of New Zealand Universities, one game before the first test, and that fateful encounter would throw the selection plans – such as they were – into further turmoil. But Billy was also to find an ally in New Zealand who would kick and cajole him into performances he had no idea he was capable of. That man was Gordon Brown – 'Broon o'Troon' as he is affectionately called throughout the rugby world. Without doubt, the Lions Tour of New Zealand in 1977 would signal the time when Beaumont finally came of age.

But all that was still in the future. First, there were domestic odds and ends to tidy up and a mere few days in which to attend to them. The holiday in Minorca was cancelled but there was no refund. The travel company, Billy remembers, were sympathetic, but illness was the only criterion for refunding a customer's money and he could hardly plead that when in less than a week he would be wearing the red jersey of the British Lions on a rugby field on the other side of the world.

Work was less of a problem. He was dedicated to his job but, as a director of the family firm of Blackledge and Sons, he was effectively his own employer, so permission from on high would not be required. Finally, on the 10th of June, 1977, two years after he had made his first, uncertain debut for England against Ireland as a last minute substitute for Roger Uttley, William Blackledge Beaumont became a fully fledged British Lion.

7

1977: LIONS AT BAY

The journey to Christchurch, New Zealand by air takes thirty-two hours. Beaumont nearly didn't make it. He got to London all right, where he collected his smart blue blazer and was on time for his rendezvous with travelling companion John Lawrence, secretary of the Four Home Unions. But then things started to go wrong.

The M4 motorway that links the capital with Heathrow Airport is notorious for traffic hold-ups. One breakdown or accident on the elevated section, for example, can set off a jam that stretches a minimum of four miles. What makes the motorway less reliable still is the sheer volume using it, both to and from the west. It turned out to be one of those days. Billy and John Lawrence were sitting on the airport bus, quietly congratulating themselves for having completed all arrangements with time to spare when the bus ground to a halt. For a while, they sat it out, checking their watches occasionally as the minutes ticked away, until it became clear that nothing less than a fleet of bulldozers was going to make any impression on this jam. They reached a grim decision – they would have to run for it.

Lawrence, a small, dapper man in his fifties with a luxuriant Battle of Britain moustache, must have looked an incongruous figure as he sprinted along the hard shoulder of the M4 waving his brolly ahead of him like a sabre. No less incongruous was the man-mountain trailing in his wake carrying two suitcases and seeming on the point of expiring. It was two miles and Billy remembers every last painful centimetre.

They finally made it to the airport and collapsed, exhausted, into their seats on the aeroplane. The story of that dramatic dash was to pass into rugby legend and receive a little embellishment along the way. The most popular version has Beaumont carrying the two suitcases *and* John Lawrence. Billy winces at the thought. 'The truth is he was so far ahead of me by the time we got to the terminal that I was having serious doubts about my fitness for the tour.'

Meanwhile, back in New Zealand, the Lions were restoring a little of their flagging morale by disposing of the powerful Southland side 20-12 at Invercargill. Gareth Evans, Elgan Rees, and Mike Gibson all ran in tries while the huge lock, Allan Martin, demonstrated his worth as a long range place kicker with two penalties. The Lions now had eight wins in a row to their credit and only one relatively easy fixture against the New Zealand Universities in Christchurch before the crucial first test in Wellington. That 'easy' game was to be the turning point of the whole tour.

Just how paper-thin the fabric of the Lions' morale had become was summed up in the few salty words of wisdom Beaumont received from the Irish Number 8, Willie Duggan, shortly after arriving. The London plane touched down a few hours before the Southland party was due back so Billy and John Lawrence were driven to the team hotel to await the conquering heroes.

When they finally arrived there were warm greetings for the newcomer and Beaumont was basking in the camaraderie when Duggan approached. He was smiling as he said, 'If I were you Billy, I'd take the next plane home.' The tour management were not amused. Duggan, as Beaumont puts it, 'received a sharp riposte and a rollicking for speaking out of turn.' Duggan had been the victim of one of the truly nasty incidents of the tour when

49

Mark Donaldson, the scrum half of Ranfurley Shield holders Manawatu, appeared to kick him deliberately in the head when Duggan became trapped at the bottom of a ruck. What incensed the Lions, and particularly their skipper Phil Bennett, was that the referee ignored the incident completely and the New Zealand press, which was becoming increasingly hostile and boorish, ignored it too.

So Duggan, whimsically or otherwise, had cause for complaint. But really, he was expressing the feeling of many of the players and it was that realisation that upset the increasingly sensitive Dawes and Burrell. The almost-constant rain was eating away at everyone's nerves, reducing leisure activities to a desultory game of cards or chess or snooker. Derek Quinnell, the brilliant Welsh back row forward who starred for the 1971 Lions in New Zealand and was expected to be a key member of this touring party as well, summed up the problem when he later remarked: 'In 1971 we played golf and in 1977 we played snooker. Which would you prefer?' Still, for Billy Beaumont, newly arrived from England and itching to get stuck in, the real tensions were buried, as yet, below the surface. The pot had been simmering a long time though, and it was the defeat by the Universities – and what followed – that caused it to finally boil over.

The Universities were captained that day by Doug Rollerson, a centre-cum-fly half of some class and uncanny perception. Later, he would become one of the more creative All Blacks of the modern era although his defection to Australia and the riches of Rugby League early in 1982 meant his career was too brief to be judged in the widest overall context.

Never mind. For now he was the young, enthusiastic brain behind a side so fit and so energetic that they ran the Lions all over the park. The pressure was suffocating and mistakes began to pile up. By half-time the Universities were 9-3 ahead and the

Lions were too demoralised to capitalise on their wider experience in the second period. As Bennett said: 'We weren't even in the game, as the students worried and harrassed us. It was a shattering blow to our pride and to our preparation for the first test match.' The final scoreline read, Universities 21, British Lions 9, and Quinnell's solitary try for the tourists was no more than a token. Doug Morgan, the scrum half, was the other scorer, converting Quinnell's effort and putting over a penalty goal of his own.

Retribution came next day. It was swift and it was terrible. Dawes assembled the whole playing party and conducted a training session of such unrelenting ferocity that for some who were there it has remained among the most vivid memories of their lives in rugby.

In his autobiography Bennett says: 'There are times when I find it difficult to remember matches or individual incidents, but when I'm old and grey I shall remember the morning after the match with the students with total clarity. It was the most painful session that I've ever encountered.'

Billy's memory is equally clear. As a newcomer, softened by the summer, he had more to do to bring his fitness up to match peak and, ironically, that torture session may have actually helped him into the test side later. Never before had he been asked to draw upon such reserves of strength and character and I think he was a little surprised to find just how much of both he really possessed. But for the rest of the players, some already battle-weary and bored, the incident was a disaster.

Was it a desperate gamble by Dawes to bring his players up to a peak of fitness for the first test, or was the coach exacting punishment? Bennett is still not sure. Beaumont is prepared to believe the former but he is equally convinced it cost the Lions the opening test as they left their fitness on the training ground, like racehorses that have been overtrained before a big race. He considers it was, at best, a serious error of judgement by Dawes and made him begin to question for the first time the Welshman's ability as a coach – something he had previously taken for granted.

The training ground was in a field near the hotel, separated from it by a shallow brook. To reach the field the players had to walk along the river bank for perhaps two hundred yards before crossing by a small bridge. The players assembled, accompanied by the usual group of Lions-watchers, and the session began. For more than an hour the players ran and exercised, ran and exercised with no break and no change in the monotonous routine. Finally, when it seemed the torment must end, Dawes ordered the group off on a half mile run. The onlookers could hardly believe their eyes. Seasoned campaigners like Allan Martin were cursing the very skies while others were simply sick on the spot.

After the run a two minute break was followed by skill sessions and press-ups. The forwards scrummaged until every muscle screamed in protest and every bone was sore from constant pressure and collision. Finally, the session ended and Beaumont found to his surprise that he was still intact. Wearily, he trudged towards the bridge and the sanctuary of the hotel – but others didn't. The two hundred yards represented too great a physical effort and they just waded silently, knee deep through the water in their track suits and training clothes.

That night found the touring party at its lowest ebb. No one had the energy for games, and humour – even gallows humour – was thin on the ground. Most simply trudged off to bed to banish the nightmare. Allan Martin, who had been almost moved to mutiny during the afternoon, found himself rewarded with a test place for the Saturday and he was one of nine Welshmen selected to face the All Blacks.

The other second row place went to Moss Keane, Brown having been ruled out by injury. They were opposed by formidable opponents – Keane by Oliver at the front of the line-out, and Martin by the outstanding Jumper Andy Haden. Theirs would be among the decisive battles and the All Blacks were destined to hold the initiative throughout. Perhaps if the Lions had won that first test, the pack would have been picked en masse for the second encounter. But they didn't and afterwards Beaumont was to sense the first glimmer of hope.

History, in the northern hemisphere at least, recalls the test as the one the Lions gave away. On the other side of the world they view things rather differently, and the opportunism of the gutsy little winger Grant Batty from Wellington is cited as the reason for victory. The fact is the lead changed hands five times and all three of the All Black tries could, and should, have been prevented.

For the first try, the All Black scrum half Sid Going found himself with the play near the Lions 22 metre line in the middle of the field and with no real attacking option. Initially, he sought to pass to his right, but then changed his mind. Next, he examined the possibility of moving the ball to his left, but that seemed covered too. Finally he decided to run straight ahead and await developments and the Lions were sufficiently mesmerised to allow him almost a clear passage. The two tackles which did go in were too weak and too late to prevent the chunky scrum half from crashing over the line.

The second try found the Lions dozing yet again. Bryan Williams, the All Black winger and place kicker, mis-hit a penalty attempt into the wind and as the ball climbed and then hung in the air, the New Zealand prop, Brad Johnstone, followed up to pressurise the defender into an error. He succeeded in making him miss the ball altogether and was able to plunge over the line close enough to the posts to allow

Williams to slot an easy conversion. Throughout the match the All Backs could claim to have the edge in the forward exchanges but strangely, the Lions still looked to have the greater capacity for penetration, and it was while they were attacking strongly that Batty popped up to change the face of the match.

The Lions had created a promising overlap and looked almost certain to score. Batty, faced with the choice of committing himself to one man in the tackle and leaving another clear, decided to hang back and he was rewarded when Trevor Evans responded to a crunching tackle by Bruce Robertson by lobbing a speculative pass inside in the general direction of Phil Bennett. Batty pounced, plucking the ball out of the air and, ignoring Bennett's despairing lunge, accelerated sixty yards to score near the posts. Williams converted and the All Blacks were suddenly four points ahead at 16-12 with half time beckoning and the advantage of using the wind in the second half.

What made the situation even more galling for the Lions was that both Irvine and Bennett were showing exceptional kicking form and, indeed, Irvine had drawn gasps from the crowd by thundering a sixty-yard penalty over for the Lions right at the beginning of the match. Bennett had added three with equal comfort and the tourists, mistakes not withstanding, looked to have the initiative.

Batty had literally snatched that initiative away. As manager George Burrell remarked wryly at the after-match dinner, Batty had scored a twelve-point try. Instead of being eight points ahead, as seemed inevitable from their attacking position, they changed ends four points behind. Beaumont and his colleagues watching from the sidelines were shattered by the sickening turn of events. J. B. G. Thomas, the foremost chronicler of Lions' tours, remarked later that the match was won and lost at the line-out, where Haden and Oliver seemed able to do as they pleased,

54

and by three incredible errors. 'Even with continuous possession,' he wrote, 'the All Blacks were so pedestrian behind the scrum against a brave Lions defence that they never really looked like scoring.'

But pedestrian or not they had the points on the board and the Lions had neither the wit nor the resource to mount a convincing response. The match petered out in the long second half. The defeat was enough in itself but there were other worries. The form of the four big men in the New Zealand line – Haden, Oliver, Laurie Knight and Ian Kirkpatrick – looked ominous for the future. But more serious still was the prospect that Bennett might not be able to take any further part in the tour.

The Lions' captain had been one of those who attempted a last ditch tackle on Sid Going. Willie Duggan had been the other, and in falling, Duggan had landed on Bennett's shoulder with a hefty thump. It is a tribute to the little Welshman's courage that he stayed on the pitch for the full eighty minutes but after the game the doctor who examined him was in favour of immobilising his shoulder by putting it in plaster.

Realising the implications of such a drastic move, Bennett demurred and the management wisely bowed to his wishes. The bruising was severe but there was just a chance that cold ice-pack treatment would work and enable him to recover in time for at least the third and fourth tests. As it turned out, he made the second test. And so did Billy Beaumont, after dragging himself back from the depths of despair against Marlborough-Nelson's Bay at Blenheim in a provincial match.

After the test defeat, there were no recriminations from John Dawes. He was as disappointed as his players at the cruel turn of events but wise enough to see that the All Blacks could be beaten if silly mistakes could be eliminated and the forwards settled and organised. There were no more torture training sessions. Instead, he appointed Terry Cobner captain in place of the injured Bennett for the next provincial game against a combined South Canterbury/Mid Canterbury/ North Otago Side. And the response was electrifying.

Cobner had been itching to get his hands on the forwards and instil some tactical cohesion into their play. His brief tenure as captain would give him an excuse to do just that and the team responded by swamping the combined side 45-6. It was just the fillip the Lions needed. Dawes took the hint and from then on, Cobner was deputed to organise training for the forwards leaving Dawes free to work on the skills of the backs. It was a move long overdue, but no less welcome for all that.

Looking back, it is surprising that the coach didn't delegate some of his massive burden earlier. The 1971 Lions under Carwyn James contained the most talented backs ever to play as a unit for the British Isles. But while the credit for success in the series has usually gone to those outside the scrum – Edwards, Dawes, Gibson, J. P. R. Williams, Davies, Duckham, plus Barry John's formidable boot – most insiders believe it could not have been achieved without the solid platform provided by the forwards. James, a prince among coaches, was astute enough to accept that no former back – he had himself been an international fly half for Wales, understudying Cliff Morgan for the most part – could truly appreciate the nuances and subtleties of forward play, even if he swallowed every coaching manual ever written on the subject. So he enlisted the thoughtful Irish prop, Ray McGlouchlan, to coach the forwards while he concerned himself with working out tactical plans and organising the backs.

The same was true of Syd Miller's all-conquering Lions in South Africa in 1974. Willie John McBride was the captain and therefore able to combine with Miller, a fellow Irishman, on all aspects of forward

56

play. (Millar had been a prop, Willie John was a peerless lock; no better combination.) But it was to the credit of Gareth Edwards, Bennett and other senior backs that the Lions' play behind the scrum was so all-conquering.

Now Dawes was getting to grips with rebuilding playing patterns in time for the second test, but first he had to solve some off-field problems that had begun to command more press attention than the games themselves.

The New Zealand sporting press, like its counterpart to the west in Australia, has never been noted for objectivity or generosity towards its sporting visitors. Now splash headlines over stories of 'hotel wrecking' and 'drunken orgies' began to appear.

The most singular of these appeared in a paper called *The Truth* and recounted an incident in a Wellington hotel when Fran Cotton and one or two other thirsty lions, 'lifted' the bar which had been inexplicably closed and shuttered one Sunday afternoon. At first, the hotel manager was angry at this bit of free enterprise but after assurances that not only would the damage be paid for but there would be a serious attempt to drink the place dry on his behalf, his mood swiftly altered to delight. As Bennett recalls: 'It was one of the more pleasant of the impromptu gatherings with the manager's till singing away to his unexpected afternoon rush.' But two days later, in the morning press, came the headline, 'Lions Wreck Hotel Bar'.

In the wake of stories such as that, relations between the players, the New Zealand press and, in some instances, the public grew bitter and strained. Again, Bennett recalls: 'We had reached the stage when the Lions were being spat upon, cans were thrown at us and the language used against us wasn't even fit for a Christchurch gutter.'

8

1977: A DREAM BECOMES REALITY

Beaumont had become a fully-fledged Lion at
Timaru. Thanks to Cobner's re-organisation and
some illegal but highly effective jumping across the
line-out, the Lions had cruised to a 45-6 win. His
second game was against West Coast Buller at
Westport and this time the Lions rattled up 45 points
without reply. It occurred to Billy that playing for the
Dirt Trackers might be quite fun after all though he
couldn't quite disguise his frustration at missing the
'big games' against Canterbury and Wellington.

His third match in New Zealand turned out to be
one of the most important of his life. The Lions were
in Blenheim, one of the loveliest parts of the country
but not noted as a rugby stronghold. Their
opponents, Marlborough-Nelson's Bay were expected
to provide the tourists with a gentle workout four
days before the second test in Christchurch. None of
the potential test backs were in the team and the
forwards contained only three certainties: Price,
Quinnell and Brown. All were included to prove their
fitness, or so Billy thought. But the choice of Brown
was in fact a tactical move on Dawes' part. He had
become so alarmed at the deterioration in the line-out
play that he was desperate to find a convincing
combination. Something told him that with
Beaumont and Brown in harness the chemistry might
come right. He was not disappointed.

Once Billy had got over the shock of finding Brown
partnering him in the no-hopers, he began to realise
he was on trial and this was potentially the most

important game of his life. Brown was as anxious for Beaumont to succeed as he was himself and kept geeing up his partner whenever he looked like flagging. Billy was playing well but beginning to feel the pace and when he turned to Brown at a scrummage to confess his discomfort, the Scot gave a reply that has passed into rugby lore. 'Billy,' he said, 'You and I are going into that test team together, come what may. And every time you slacken off or opt out of anything in the next twenty minutes I'm going to belt you as hard as I can!'

At the end, Dawes was satisfied. He had found his second row combination. In all, the Lions made six changes for that crucial second test. Apart from Beaumont, Quinnell came in on the flank; Fran Cotton replaced Phil Orr at loosehead prop, and Peter Wheeler won the vote over Bobby Windsor for the key hooking spot. This was to be particularly significant for Beaumont, who was used to Wheeler's throw in at the line-out. Gareth Evans also won his first cap, replacing England's Peter Squires on the wing, and that was the only change that seemed unjustified.

The All Blacks were unwilling to disturb their successful side. Duncan Robertson was the only casualty of the first test, Doug Bruce taking his place in the centre. But their careful plans were quickly thwarted when Grant Batty, interception hero of the Wellington match, decided his suspect knee was no longer up to the rigours of test match rugby and not only withdrew from the side but announced his retirement from the game. It was the kind of blow that had 'ill omen' written all over it. Batty had been one of the truly great All Blacks, scoring forty-five tries in fifty-six matches and earning the universal rating as the best left wing in the world. Only he had been aware that his playing days were numbered when he took the field in that opening test. He was a small man, quick and brave, and had received plenty of

59

punishment in his career. Now his knee had given up and, wisely, he elected to retire on one of the highest points of achievement. There were other blows to follow for New Zealand, most serious in the context of what would follow being the withdrawal of Bruce Robertson to be replaced in the centre by Bill Osborne. Then Lambert, the prop, was taken ill with suspected appendicitis and back came the talented, but still raw, Maori Billy Bush.

Cobner's influence on the Lions was to show early on. Suddenly, these clean cut poms began barging and jumping across in the line-outs instead of straight up and down. It was the technique which had been first tried at Timaru and Billy Beaumont had become well versed in its dubious arts.

At first, the All Blacks were perplexed. They had become used to monopolising this illegal aspect of play under benign, perhaps unknowing, referees. But the Lions proved, if anything, more adept and though it was messy to look at and certainly offended the purists, it soon proved highly effective. Beaumont, while rarely winning clean ball, dominated his opposite number at the front of the line-out, Frank Oliver, and the Lions gleaned enough possession to allow the 'sweeper' Quinnell to tidy up. And when the ball was thrown to the middle of the line, Gordon Brown timed his jumps to such effect that the bigger man, Andy Haden, was left clutching at thin air.

This new control and confidence among the Lions forwards soon spilled over to the backs. Phil Bennett kicked with such precision that New Zealand were pinned back in their own half for long periods: defending was both tiring and demoralising. Worse still for the All Blacks, the Lions' captain was having one of those 'eye of the needle' days with his place kicks so by half time, New Zealand were thirteen points to six adrift. Bennett had even manufactured the try by J. J. Williams, chipping astutely ahead to set McGeechan on a run which ended with the Scot dummying new cap Mark Taylor and going over for a try in the corner. The conversion was well struck but spun off the upright.

The second half was brutal. Kevin Eveleigh, the All Blacks' flanker, took it upon himself to administer punishment on both Graham Price and Bennett. The Lions' captain was late-tackled and a brawl ensued; Price was literally pinioned by scrum-half Sid Going while Eveleigh seemed to pound him with a fist. Yet the referee, Mr Duffy of Taranaki, making an inauspicious debut with the whistle, seemed oblivious to the escalating violence. The Lions didn't score after half time but the All Blacks did, Bryan Williams kicking a penalty which at 13-9 put them within a fingertip of victory.

For the Lions, lightning almost struck twice. As the clock ticked agonisingly towards no side, Osborne worked a neat scissors with Sid Going in the centre of the field and, having drawn the Lions' centres, Fenwick and McGeechan, threw out a high pass to Jaffray. The Otago man was going at full speed and as he juggled to control the ball, Gareth Evans came in to tackle. Jaffray lost his battle with the law of gravity as he crossed the line and as the ball spun on to the turf, so Evans threw himself on to it to claim a drop out. Seconds later, the whistle blew and the once demoralised Lions were truly back in the hunt.

In the dressing room afterwards, Beaumont eased himself gingerly on to a bench and surveyed the scene around him. Every muscle in his body ached and his eyes were almost glued shut by the mud. But his hearing was fully intact and Welsh and Irish voices were in full song as they proclaimed the famous victory. The room, he recalls, resembled a casualty station but there was no mistaking the mood of elation as the champagne flowed freely. Never before had the Lions won a test at Lancaster Park, nor, for that matter, the second test in any series in New

Zealand. At last it seemed the ill-fated tour had turned the corner.

After the rigours of the battle, Billy was given a well-earned breather. Moss Keane and Allan Martin resumed their partnership in the second row against the Maoris at Eden Park, Auckland, and Billy became a spectator at one of the most exciting matches of the whole tour. It was also one of the friendliest, in sharp contrast to the events in Christchurch and resulted in a breathtaking 22-19 win for the Lions over Sid Going's adventurous side.

Brown and Beaumont were back together for the eighteenth match of the tour against Waikato in Hamilton and that game was memorable for a quite different reason. The sun shone! The ground was firm, the gentle breeze was refreshing and the Lions put on a virtuoso display behind the pack with Brynmor Williams calling the tune. The final score was close, 18-13 to the tourists after they had trailed 4-7 at half time, but they were never in any real danger of losing. Williams hit a peak in this match and New Zealand supporters watched with growing concern the little man darting hither and thither. He had already proved a staunch match for their hero Going in the opening two tests and now it seemed he was ready to swamp him. Sadly, Williams never finished the game. He tore a hamstring in the second half and although he stayed on the field until the final few minutes, he was virtually a passenger.

The Lions management were anxious to play down the extent of Williams' injury knowing full well that the New Zealand selectors were toying with the idea of replacing Going with the quick passing Lyn Davis for the third test. There was no doubt in the minds of either Dawes or Bennett which was the greater danger to the Lions: Going was a master tactician and strongman, in the Gareth Edwards mould, but he was something of a loner and could be contained. With Davis in the side, the Lions could expect greater pressure on their threequarters and the prospect didn't have much appeal.

The run up to the third test saw the Lions at their very best, especially in the game against Auckland (which many thought they might lose) and, injuries notwithstanding, they were now in good heart. The smear stories continued but the Lions had closed ranks and become immune to the campaign of lies and innuendo in some sections of the New Zealand press.

As expected, Beaumont and Brown were again teamed up in the second row and on paper, the team of Irvine (full back), J. J. Williams, Evans (wings), Burcher, Fenwick (centres), Bennett (fly half and captain), Brynmor Williams (scrum half), Cotton, Price (props), Wheeler (hooker), Beaumont, Brown (locks), Quinnell, Cobner (flankers) and Duggan (Number 8) was their strongest combination. McGeechan had lost form in the centre and Burcher, growing in stature with every game, seemed to strengthen the side by his inclusion rather than weaken it. But there were niggling injuries to key players and the cynics were already speculating on which of them would last the distance. A soft, wet ground is no place for a man with a serious muscle injury and the fitness test on Brynmor Williams had been as inconclusive as it had been perfunctory. With Doug Morgan also nursing a strain, Dawes elected to gamble.

The 'Drop Going' campaign bore fruit. Not only did the All Blacks bring in Davis at scrum half but they made five other changes as well. On the face of it they seemed like panic moves but New Zealand coach Jackie Gleeson, wily old fox that he was, was merely acting on the 'horses for courses' principle and bringing in men to do a specific job. One was Graham Mourie, the Taranaki flanker, winning his first cap. He and Beaumont were to meet several times in the years that followed and each was to prove in his own

63

quiet, undemonstrative way an outstanding captain.

Just as Christchurch and the second test had been the high water mark of Beaumont's tour, Dunedin was to be its trough. The game was barely a minute old when Beaumont, leaping across Oliver at the front of a line-out, deflected the ball into the hands of the All Black winger Brian Ford. New Zealand quickly set up a ruck, sucking in the Lions' cover and, having won the ball, Davis whipped a fast, accurate pass out to his threequarters. The Lions, caught on the wrong foot, failed to kill a neat chip forward by centre Bruce Robertson and Kirkpatrick gathered the loose ball on the tourists' line to score. New full back Bevan Wilson converted and it was six nil to the All Blacks.

Andy Irvine did his best to pull the Lions straight back into the game when he came agonisingly close to landing a 50-yard penalty but although they didn't score that time, the Lions took comfort from his confident aggression, and slowly but surely began to gather momentum. The match was still only six minutes old when Bennett placed a beautiful kick into touch five yards from the New Zealand goal line. With the All Blacks to throw, it was up to the Lions to pressurise their opponents and make sure that any ball they won was thoroughly bad ball. They succeeded admirably with Beaumont making amends for his earlier mistake by spoiling Oliver's jump and helping his side win the put in at a set scrum. It was just the platform Brynmor Williams had hoped for. The little Welshman collected Wheeler's quick, sharp strike and darted around the blindside where he found Duggan breaking in support. Williams was held up but Duggan had the momentum to claw his way through the defence for a morale-boosting try. Surprisingly, Bennett missed the conversion.

If the Lions had been able to tighten the screw then, New Zealand might have been locked out of the game altogether, but Bennett's missed conversion was a sign of things to come. The captain began to lose the range of his touch finding kicks as well and with All Black skipper Tane Norton leading his men by example with fiery work in the loose, the Lions were harried into making simple mistakes.

Beaumont noted with growing dismay the jitters affecting his colleagues behind the scrum. Passes were dropped or fumbled as the New Zealand back row, with Mourie leading the way, surged on to the attack. It was galling for the forwards who still controlled the tight to see a stream of possession mis-used, and as the mistakes multiplied, Bennett and the rest seemed to lose all perspective. New Zealand could hardly believe their luck when a pressure-relieving Lions drop-out on the twenty-two yard line turned into a set scrum as a Lions back carelessly wandered ahead of the kicker. Norton struck beautifully in the front row; the ball was moved quickly onwards by Bruce and Ford on the blindside and the All Blacks piled in to win the ruck and allow Haden to get a hand on the ball over the visitors' line. It was a try quite out of the blue and one that would effectively end the contest.

It was downhill all the way from then on. First J. J. Williams limped off with a leg injury, to be replaced by McGeechan with Gareth Evans switching to the right wing. And then, early in the second half, Brynmor Williams finally conceded defeat to his torn hamstring and Doug Morgan came on to take his place at scrum half. Still the mistakes multiplied. New Zealand were allowed to add three more penalties against one for the Lions to take their score to 19-7. That was how it finished. After the thrill of winning the second test on his debut, Billy was brought back to earth with a resounding bump. There were to be no more paydays that counted. And indeed, the fourth and final test was to prove the bitterest of all.

Injuries are a regrettable fact of touring life, but now they began to dominate conversation and depress the shattered Lions still further. The loss of

Williams was felt most keenly. Somehow the ebullient Welshman had come to epitomise the never-say-die philosophy of the beleaguered touring party, but with Morgan – another diehard – by no means at the peak of fitness, the management wisely decided to send for a replacement. He was Alun Lewis of London Welsh, a darting, all-action half back but like so many of the Lions, inexperienced at the highest level. On the other hand, Charlie Faulkner of Pontypool who was also flown in to replace Clive Williams at loosehead prop, had bags of experience. With Graham Price and Bobby Windsor, he was one of the legendary Pontypool Front Row; a fierce scrummager if less than sprightly in the loose; he was in the twilight of a glittering career.

The walking wounded included Mike Gibson and Bruce Hay but, in the context of the final test match, more serious were the doubts about pack leader Terry Cobner, flanker Derek Quinnell and the flying winger J. J. Williams. When those doubts became reality, Tony Neary of England was called up along with the young Newport flanker, Jeff Squire, while Elgan Rees took over from J.J.

The fifteen men who finally took the field at Eden Park, Auckland on August 13, 1977 – Beaumont amongst them – needed no exhortation from coach or captain to motivate them. Beaumont, in particular, had tuned himself to a high pitch. He was an established lock now, one of the best New Zealand rugby watchers had seen and they were warm in their praise. Sid Going nominated Beaumont and Peter Wheeler as the stars of the Lions pack and in a wry postscript was to add: 'It made you wonder how many other good players were left behind just because they weren't Welshmen.'

For once, match conditions were perfect. 'Weather sunny, ground firm' was the official statement of the going which also noted a sell-out crowd of 58,000 packed into the historic ground. Bennett, viewing the 'freak' conditions, was optimistic and for forty minutes his optimism was gloriously justified.

When Bevan Wilson opened the scoring for the All Blacks with a penalty after the Lions' backs had wandered carelessly offside, there was no hint of depression in the visitors' camp. The forwards were winning everything up front and what possession came New Zealand's way was so meagre as to appear negligible. And then, when Morgan equalised the scores after twenty-five minutes and then ran in, and converted a fine try, an avalanche seemed on the cards. The much vaunted New Zealand pack had conceded the forward battle to such an extent that on one occasion they packed only the front three in a scrummage, pulling back locks and flankers to defend. As Billy admits, 'It made us feel like kings.' But it had technical disadvantages (and, incidentally, is no longer legal) because the laws state that no side shall shove until the ball is into the scrum. With only the front row in position, the ball was in and out of the New Zealand put-in so fast that the Lions couldn't capitalise on their huge weight advantage.

Still, with the ball available to them almost constantly throughout the half, the Lions only turned 9-3 to the good, and Beaumont was acutely conscious of just how fragile that lead could prove in an exchange of penalties. His concern was amply justified. A spell of All Black pressure early in the second half saw the home side camped inside the Lions twenty-two and a technical offence in a set scrum – right in front of the posts – gave Wilson the simplest of kicks to reduce the lead.

Twice more the Lions had opportunities to make the match safe but Morgan, the nine points hero of the first forty minutes, suddenly lost his range and New Zealand remained tantalisingly in touch. It was finally Bennett who set up the winning score – but tragically, for the New Zealanders. He describes the cruel finale:

'From a scrum the All Blacks hoisted a high kick. Going underneath it, I fielded it and my first thoughts were of a long driving kick back into their territory. There was that need to keep them away from an attacking position. However, the kick went towards Bill Osborne and he seized upon the chance to put more pressure on the Lions' line with another kick down into our own twenty-two. Steve Fenwick got underneath this one and fed Peter Wheeler the hooker. Wheeler was tackled by Mourie, the ball went loose into Knight's hands and he went for the corner. They had won the series by three games to one and we had lost this one by a point. God, I felt sick!'

Two images remain vivid in Billy's mind from that desperate last five minutes. Tears rolling down Bennett's cheeks as he realised the full import of the defeat and the look of horror and bewilderment on the face of the Lions hooker as Fenwick lobbed that suicidal pass. The All Blacks captain Tane Norton promptly announced his retirement from international rugby after the match. He had held the hooking position since 1971.

Needless to say, post match celebrations in the Lions' camp were muted. Phil Bennett could hardly bring himself to face his shattered colleagues in the dressing room while for John Dawes it was simply a nightmare. Beaumont could at least temper his frustration by the knowledge that he had had a marvellous tour. He had completely dominated his opposite number, Frank Oliver, in each of the three tests and found a level of commitment and fitness he hadn't known he possessed.

The final, abiding memory of New Zealand for Billy and all his team mates came next day at the airport. As the plane climbed sluggishly into the sullen, southern skies, a cheer went up from the Lions party that might have been heard in London. The war was over. But for Billy Beaumont the domestic battles lay ahead.

9

1978: CAPTAIN AT LAST!

Beaumont returned to England with his star in the ascendent. As a senior Lion he became an automatic selection for the Queen's Silver Jubilee match against the Barbarians at Twickenham. His improvement and confidence were obvious from the start and with the Lions winning a rousing, running match 23-14, it was a happy homecoming.

But the off-field politics that had dogged the touring party didn't leave the players now and the public were unaware of just how close rugby came to its first 'players' strike' over the thorny question of wives and girlfriends being part of the celebrations. Phil Bennett maintains that an ultimatum was issued when the organising committee refused to allow the wives and girlfriends to join the players until after the banquet on the Saturday of the match. Yet the players' presence was requested from the Thursday and they were to be housed at the fashionable Hilton Hotel. This was too much and while the showpiece game was probably never in any real peril, the rugby authorities climbed down to the extent of agreeing to the long weekend *a deux* as long as the team accepted more modest accommodation, the Richmond Hill Hotel, close to Twickenham, as it happens, but a million miles away from the bright lights and shopping of the West End.

Even that petty irritation failed to cloud Billy's enjoyment of the occasion which meant so much to a committed royalist like himself. He recalls being presented to Prince Charles before the match as a particular highlight, especially when the heir to the throne congratulated him on being shrewd enough to create his own trademark – the distinctive white headband. 'Was it to keep his ears warm?' asked the Prince, tongue firmly in his cheek.

After the rigours of New Zealand, Beaumont was ready to take a sabbatical from international rugby; to catch up on the mountain of paperwork that had accumulated during his absence from the firm and build himself up slowly for the Home Championship matches that lay ahead. But there was to be no respite. His experience was needed to bolster the experimental England side chosen to take on the U.S. Eagles in a 'non-international' game. No caps would be awarded to the home side.

Happy as ever to oblige, Billy accepted the invitation from Malcolm Phillips, the England representative. But Phillips also had a surprise in store – 'Would Billy agree to captain the side?' He was flabbergasted. Not since the heady days as fly half at Cressbrook Primary School had he captained a rugby team and now he was being asked to lead the national side. It was the second time Malcolm Phillips had been the bearer of tidings that would radically alter the shape of his career.

The Eagles were no match for even a scratch England fifteen and went down 37-11. It was a far from strenuous test for the captain but his manner and demeanour obviously made an impression. Soon afterwards he was asked to lead the North of England in the Inter-Divisional Championship against London, and then to remain in charge for the final against the Midlands. Both games were won, the second 22-7, and again, Beaumont the captain won plaudits. Pleased though he was with this taste of the high life he remained unambitious in his role and confined his preparation to making the senior side for the final England trial. But again he found himself in charge of the senior side and despite the drabness of the match (15-15 with the Rest scoring the only try), William Blackledge Beaumont was named captain against France in the first Home international of the 1978 season.

England's selectors had made one of the shrewdest moves of their brief tenure. They had appointed a man who led by example and would, over the years, instil in each side he led a patriotism and will to win that had in recent memory been the province of Wales, Ireland and Scotland. But it was a job Billy was to grow into. There was no instant, illuminating success. Instead, France emerged winners in Paris by fifteen points to six, a scoreline that was considered 'reasonable' by those whose vision was less than expansive. Beaumont was not of their number. He was realistic enough to appreciate that France at that time had more talent at their disposal but, he reveals, he had no time for the 'we can't beat them so we might as well throw it about' brigade. Instead, in his team talk before the match he asserted his authority quite plainly when he announced England's tactics would be built on containment: 'if the French want to win, they will have to work hard for it,' he told his team.

It would be an exaggeration to say England played well enough to win. But they showed resilience and extraordinary courage when injury robbed them first of centre Andy Maxwell and then of Peter Dixon. Both replacements were on the field when prop Robin Cowling dislocated a collar bone – but he refused to go off. If you are a back, you can perhaps nurse an injury, staying out of the action as much as possible and making a contribution on the strength of your nuisance value. But not at prop, where limbs collide at each scrummage with a force that would make a weightlifter wince. Beaumont recalls Cowling's bravery that day as heroic and the selectors recognised that Beaumont had created a spirit in the side that made such bravery possible. They had no

71

hesitation in naming Billy to lead England next time out, this time against Wales at Twickenham.

Alan Old's yo-yo career continued. He was left out of the side in favour of Bath's John Horton despite the fact that his two drop goals had provided England's only score in Paris. Cowling, out for the season, was replaced by Barry Nelmes and Bob Mordell came in for the injured Peter Dixon.

Wales were used to trouncing England, home or away, but this time they got through only on the strength of Phil Bennett's boot, winning 9-6 – three penalties to two. Conditions were so bad with rain turning the pitch into a mudbath that an open handling game was out of the question, even for the talented Welsh. Billy accepted the defeat with good grace even though the England full back, Alistair Hignell, had had a relatively simple chance to force a draw. But losing rankled him. He wanted to lead a winning England side, playing to its full potential and he was determined that Scotland and Ireland would pay for the success of France and Wales.

Scotland were not at their best. In fact, they were experiencing the kind of trough that England had known in the mid-seventies. Yet a Calcutta Cup match is always a bit special to them and there was no room for complacency as Billy led his team out for the first time at Murrayfield in front of a packed house. In those days, threequarters of the pitch was surrounded by terracing and the wall of sound that poured from well lubricated Scottish throats was enough to chill the blood. Fortunately, England had been able to stiffen their pack with the recall of Cotton and Dixon and their experience and power helped the forwards to take the game by the scruff of the neck. Two tries, both converted, and a penalty by Paul Dodge gave England a heartening 15-0 win and Dodge's effort was especially noteworthy. England were leading 6-0 at the time but the infringement by Scotland which gave the visitors the penalty was fully sixty yards out. Billy was aware that neither full back David Caplan nor scrum half Malcolm Young, the two recognised place kickers, possessed heavy artillery, but he suspected the young centre, Dodge, did. He threw him the ball and the Leicester man responded perfectly.

The winning speech Beaumont gave after the dinner may not have been one of his finest or wittiest, but the fact that it was his first in a long line made it especially memorable. He was to follow it a fortnight later when England concluded an up and down season with a 15-9 win over Ireland in Dublin. After that, he could put his notes away for a while.

England did not fulfil their promise. Two tours were scheduled for the second half of 1978, one a short visit by Argentina, the other a major one by New Zealand. The All Blacks, led by Graham Mourie, would achieve the first clean sweep of Britain in that country's rugby history. And they were a good side. Not so the Argentinians. They were skilled in some departments, notably outside the scrum, but technically weak and far from experienced against top European nations. The North, led by Beaumont, gave them a pasting, but England could only manage a miserable 13-13 draw.

What should have been a taster for Home Championship successes turned flat and sour and the selectors – not for the first time in history – panicked, picking a side with good players out of position. John Scott, who had played for Rosslyn Park at lock but preferred Number 8, was picked to partner Beaumont in the second row. That allowed Roger Uttley to come into the side at Number 8 but, according to Beaumont, he was barely fit after only just recovering from injury. Fran Cotton had torn an achilles tendon right at the start of the season and could not play, so Nelmes, who had scored a try against Scotland, was asked to switch from loose head prop to tight head. He was given one of the most uncomfortable afternoons of his life. There was no hiding place where these All Blacks were concerned. Only the very best playing at their best could hope to hold them and England's lopsided pack were given a thrashing. New Zealand won 16-6 going away and the axe was poised to fall in a quite unexpected direction.

Beaumont was relieved of the captaincy. Roger Uttley was chosen to lead the senior side in the Trial. It is astounding to consider just how often these two fine players influenced and dominated one another's careers: from 1975, right through to 1979, they would criss-cross, with Uttley always seeming to draw the winning card only to see it blown away by a sudden stray gust. The new season was typical.

Although now reduced to the ranks, Billy was still considered the first choice lock in England. He lined up in the senior side for the Final Trial – split, curiously, not into two halves but three periods – and by the end of the second, he found himself back in charge again. Uttley bruised a thigh and was forced to go off. But when the England team to play Scotland in the opening Championship match at Twickenham was announced the captain was – Roger Uttley!

The saga continued. England won everything against the Scots but the match. New fly half Neil Bennett missed four reasonable shots at goal and the Scots came away from London with a 7-7 draw. Uttley didn't finish the match. Ten minutes from the end he suffered a leg injury and once again, Beaumont took over as captain. End of story? Not quite. Ireland were next on the list and when the England team was announced, there, once more with the asterisk next to his name in the papers, was Roger Uttley.

Billy was perplexed. He admired Uttley as a player *and* as a captain but he couldn't follow the logic of the selectors in picking first himself, then Uttley, then himself ad infinitum. What kind of leadership were they looking for? And how, in any case, were they different? The question was finally resolved – and I do mean finally – on the morning of the Irish match. Roger Uttley came down with flu, withdrew from the game and Beaumont took over until the end of his career.

It wasn't quite a happy ending because England played badly in Dublin and lost 15-6. Billy considers he made the first serious error of judgement in his international career during that game, heeding the wishes of the selectors to play with the strong wind in the first half should he win the toss instead of against, as he and the players wanted. He did win the toss and followed instructions, but the players were unhappy and their performance showed it. It was, he recalls, the last time he trusted anyone's judgement over his own.

The third match against the French saw England back on the winning trail. It was a tight affair with England in control up front but always under pressure against the talented French backs. But they held them at bay, and a try and a penalty enabled England to squeeze home 7-6. A disappointing international season ended with a heavy defeat against Wales in Cardiff but at least Beaumont was established as leader of the side again and there were bluer skies on the horizon.

It was time for a change of selectors and Budge Rogers, a great flanker for England and Bedford in the sixties, became chairman. Peter Colston was replaced as coach by Mike Davis, a former lock for England who had been outstandingly successful with English schools sides. Both men were committed to two things: continuity of selection and attacking from strength. In England's case, that meant building a forward base and, if you like, working backwards from there. Billy didn't need convincing that the current strength of English rugby lay up front, and with a tour of the Far East lined up for the close season, he could sense the dawning of a new era.

75

10

1979: A NEW BROOM

With a new coach and a new attitude, there was real optimism in England quarters. The Far East tour was seen as a perfect vehicle to shape a side for the eighties in a relaxed, constructive atmosphere. But it wasn't all sweetness and light. At least, not at first. Billy remembers Mike Davis striking a rather school-masterish pose – a clear legacy of his days coaching England's youngsters – and it irked some of the senior players. But to his credit, Davis was quick to spot his own shortcomings and by the end of the tour his transformation was as dramatic and complete as a chrysallis becoming a butterfly.

On the field, the tourists began rather complacently. Japan B were easily disposed of, 36-7 in the opening game, but in the second game, against the full Japanese side in Osaka, the unthinkable nearly happened. With minutes of a rip-roaring but thoroughly erratic encounter remaining, the home side led 19-15 and the rising sun seemed about to achieve its zenith. It was only the vast experience of winger Peter Squires coupled with full back Dusty Hare's reliable boot that spared England's blushes, the former with an opportunist try, the latter with a neat conversion. Beaumont was grinning with relief as he led his warriors from the field.

The Japanese had proved to be extremely resourceful and astonishingly fit. They used every conceivable ploy to nullify the huge weight advantage of the England forwards with their tiny scrum packing so low and so tightly that England were never able to shove them off the ball. In defence, they tackled fiercely, sometimes bounced off, but rose swiftly to tackle again – and if necessary, again. Finally, they were prepared to run all day and at this early stage of the tour, not all the England players seemed prepared to match that level of commitment.

In the end, England's growing organisation and monumental experience proved decisive. The second international in Tokyo was won with ease, 38-18, and England moved on to Fiji with their 100 per cent record intact. The South Seas islanders proved as much of a revelation but for quite different reasons. The carefree, uninhibited running and handling style that normally characterises their play was replaced by a dour determination to match and beat their visitors in the forward battles. Physically, they were equipped for just that, but technically, they were light years behind.

England swamped the full Fijian side 19-7 in Nadi and were equally in control against the Juniors, 39-22, in Suva. The final match of the tour against Tonga was memorable not so much for the quality of the play but for the state of the pitch which was so cratered it resembled a lunar landscape. England's mild but apprehensive protests were met with warm smiles and typical South Seas resourcefulness. By the morning of the game, the holes had all been filled in – but not with earth or sand. Instead, they housed raw coal and shingle, and most of the England backs contrived to stay on their feet throughout the match! The Tongans gave their usual carefree display and were good value for their nineteen points. But England scored thirty-seven without extending themselves to bring their final points tally to an impressive 270 for, ninety-three against on the complete tour.

Apart from being an outstanding social success, England's Far East excursion had a number of positive benefits on the playing side. New stars emerged in the back division with fly half Huw Davies and scrum half Ian Peck prominent. On the wing, John Carleton proved he had real class and it became clear that England's most successful player ever in that position, Peter Squires, was facing the biggest challenge of his career. Billy was pleased, too, at the emergence of Maurice Colclough at lock. It meant that England now had potentially two ball-winning jumpers in the middle of the line-out (Nigel Horton was the other) and with his own form having held up so well, he began to see the makings of a tough and talented England side.

Mike Davis had been given the best possible baptism in his new role as coach. The relative weakness of the opposition gave him the chance to experiment fully with the composition of each side and while by nature he was attack-minded, he knew the value of ten-man rugby as well as anyone else. The chairman of selectors and tour manager, Budge Rogers, proved popular with the players not only because he was an engaging personality but because he was in tune with their problems. His illustrious career as a flank forward had spanned a full decade. He had last played against Wales at the tail end of 1969 and he'd seen England squander talent throughout the seventies with poor planning and selectorial insensitivity. He was determined that in his reign at the top no similar charges could be laid against the committee. And finally, and crucially, it became clear that Rogers, Davis and Billy Beaumont were on exactly the same wavelength.

It is curious given the volatile nature of such things just how solidly Billy had now established himself as England captain in the public consciousness. Even the press began to take it for granted. Vivian Jenkins, the most respected voice in rugby, saw in Beaumont the model for players at every level of the game. In his monthly column in *Rugby World* in July, 1979, he wrote:

'Billy Beaumont, England's captain, covered himself in glory on his team's tour of Japan, Fiji and Tonga. Against Fiji especially, he seems to have played an outstanding game. Yet not so long ago he was just an average county forward, turning out for Lancashire and playing his heart out, but without looking, at that stage, as though he would hit the high spots in the game. Since then, however, he has fought his way into the national side (as a last minute replacement against Ireland when Roger Uttley was injured) and touring abroad, with England to Australia in 1975 and with the Lions, again as a replacement, to New Zealand in 1977.

'On the way he has collected twenty-one caps and is now firmly in the saddle as captain of the national side. What has impressed me most about his progress is the way he has responded to every succeeding challenge, often when not everyone thought he could. When he was sent out to New Zealand as a replacement for the injured Nigel Horton, for instance, few thought that within three weeks he would have won his place in the side for the internationals, and retained it to the end of the tour. As England's captain, again, his stature has increased with every match.

'It is a tribute to his personality, and will to succeed, as much as to playing ability; but it also underlines for players everywhere that to improve at any game there is nothing like having to face up to new and demanding situations. Beaumont has looked a better player with each succeeding match. His old school, Ellesmere College, and club, Fylde, can bask in his reflected glory.'

There is no doubt that in the summer of 1979 the Beaumont balance sheet was showing a healthy credit. Fylde had done more than bask in his reflected glory. Under their versatile captain, Micky Weir, and

79

with Billy working as hard for his club on a winter Saturday as he did for his country, the Lancashire side compiled a 28-8 record which included third place in the Northern Merit Table behind Liverpool and traditional rivals, Orrell. No team came away from the Woodlands Memorial Ground, Lytham, with a win that season.

As for Billy's international career, it had taken off to such an extent that he was closing in on John Currie's record of twenty-six caps for England at lock; he had won over all critics of his style of captaincy and indeed, David Frost of *The Guardian* wrote after the Far East tour:

'The tour also had another important benefit for England's immediate future. This was the development of Billy Beaumont as captain. Many people had doubts about Beaumont in this role at home, but on tour, he matured remarkably as a leader both on and off the field. It enabled him to gain the respect of everyone in the touring party.'

But the greatest challenges still lay ahead. The Far East tour had certainly answered many questions but the chain that was to link England's performances and lead to the Grand Slam of '82 was forged not in the Pacific but in the clear, crisp air of the High Veldt in South Africa.

Billy had barely unpacked his suitcase when he was off on his travels again, this time with North West Counties, and for once, Hilary was not destined to remain a rugby widow. Not only did she accompany her husband but had her eyes well and truly opened to the dedication a touring side needs if it is to be successful. Not beer and skittles, friendly tour though it was, but a grafting slog across the southern half of the African continent with suitcases forever being packed and unpacked and fresh laundry prized as highly as gold.

The party was coached by Lancashire's Des Seabrook and he had at his disposal some of the finest players in England. The half backs were Steve Smith and John Horton; Fran Cotton, Peter Dixon, Beaumont, Tony Neary and Roger Uttley were among the forwards and the threequarters included wingers John Carleton and Mike Slemen plus the crash-tackling centre Tony Bond. It was a tough party and it needed to be because the opposition comprised all the major South African provinces plus Zimbabwe (then Rhodesia). The iron-hard pitches took a heavy toll.

But not only did Beaumont and his colleagues survive the rigours of touring South Africa, they returned fitter and leaner, welded by a fierce determination. The Smith-Horton combination in particular proved a revelation.

Under the constant cajoling of his friend and mentor, Fran Cotton, Smith finally began to take himself seriously as a rugby player. He lost pounds in excess weight, developed a longer, quicker pass and thus gave Horton time and space to demonstrate his nimble footwork. Both Seabrook and Beaumont could sense an England partnership in the making although Billy was still a committed advocate of Alan Old as England's fly half. As for Cotton himself, he had been virtually a spectator in the previous twelve months as a damaged achilles tendon refused to respond to treatment. The trip gave him an opportunity to test his recovery away from the beady eyes of England's selectors and press.

Billy had become well versed by now in the tactic of driving in and rolling off from the ensuing mauls. It required fast flank forwards to make it effective and they had to be good ball carriers too. Dixon, Uttley and Neary matched all the requirements and so effective was the ploy that the chairman of the Northern Division selectors, Mike Weston, would go out of his way to pick only those players who could operate within Seabrook's tactical plan for the prestige match against the All Blacks on their 1979 tour of Scotland and England.

That would be an historic game, but equally historic in its way was the naming of Billy Beaumont to captain England in the international match at Twickenham fully a month before the game. Equally unprecedented was the decision of Budge Rogers and Mike Davis to invite their captain down to London for informal discussions on the composition of the side. Times were certainly changing.

So determined was Seabrook's Northern squad to beat the New Zealanders that they began meeting once a week for squad training in the middle of October. The match was scheduled for Otley on November 17, one week before the Twickenham international. And the first thing everyone agreed on was that Alan Old, the Yorkshire fly half so badly misused by England over the previous season, would be the key to their strategy. His place kicking skills were a matter of record, but it was his control and ability to dictate the play which were considered his prime assets, enabling the North to play a tight, spoiling game.

In the second row, Beaumont was to be partnered by Jim Sydall of Waterloo, a tough, unflappable character already on the verge of England honours. Sydall was no line-out gazelle but neither was he likely to be deflected from his task. His opponent would be the giant Andy Haden, one of the finds of New Zealand rugby and perhaps the most talented lock that country has produced since the great Colin Meads. At the end of the day it was the imperious Haden who would be taken to the cleaners.

New Zealand arrived in Otley with their 100 per cent record intact. Scotland had been soundly beaten 20-6 at Murrayfield and Mourie's All Blacks seemed well on course to repeat their Grand Slam achievement of 1978 – the first time a New Zealand team had won every match. But in deference to the strength of the Northern squad Mourie elected to field his 'international side' instead of giving some of the overworked stalwarts like flankers Murray Mexted and Ken Stewart a well earned rest. The trio had cut attacking aspirations to shreds. The Midlands Division, for example, had sent out some of the best runners in English rugby – Dodge, Woodward, Perry, Cusworth – and been slaughtered 33-7. On paper the North appeared equally well served behind the scrum with Carleton and Slemen on the wings and the tricky Tony Wright at outside centre. But Tony Bond was earmarked for the key role. If New Zealand had known they would be facing the most devastating, committed tackler in the English game they might not have sent out a running fly half like Eddie Dunn.

When Billy arrived for the game he was delighted to find the rain that had trailed him from Chorley was making a fine old mess of the pitch at Otley. It pounded into the turf like machine gun fire, egged on by a stinging wind that bent the trees and threatened the security of the adventurers perched precariously in their branches. A forward battle was now inevitable and Billy and his boys were ready.

11

1979: ALL BLACK BLUES

New Zealand won the toss and chose to attack with the gale at their backs, a tactic approved of by most modern captains but one that must be exploited to the full. They made a sluggish start. Richard Wilson, the full back, had several good chances to put his side into a commanding lead as the North conceded penalty after penalty in their anxiety to command the forward play. Beaumont eventually settled them, aided and abetted by Alan Old's precise kicking, and the score sheet remained blank as half time approached.

Billy would gladly have settled for nil-nil at the interval but Richard Wilson provided an unexpected bonus when he, and his namesake, the winger Stuart Wilson, made a mess of gathering Steve Smith's diagonal kick. A full back usually takes responsibility for a fifty-fifty ball but on this occasion, Richard Wilson did not call. Stuart Wilson hesitated and Mike Slemen, following up with pace, stole the awkward bounce. His pass back inside found Smith and the scrum half scrambled over the line. Old's conversion into the wind missed narrowly, but minutes later, the All Black's conceded a penalty and, this time, Old got the ball over. When the whistle sounded, Beaumont's men found themselves holding an improbable 7-0 lead.

Stunned by the reverse, the All Blacks raised their game as the second half got under way and the North had to defend desperately to keep them at bay. Gradually, though, their forwards regained the initiative and Mourie's men were reduced to playing without the ball.

As Beaumont and his men drove forward, rolled off from the mauls to suck in the New Zealand back row, and then drove forward again, it became clear that their tactical plan was draining the strength and energy from the visitors. Even Mourie had lost his crucial edge of speed. And it was at that point that the North's backs began to open out.

Tony Bond showed that his power and commitment was by no means confined to knocking people over. He showed speed in attack, coupled with some clever footwork and ran in two tries that sent shock waves rolling around the ground. Old converted one to give the North a 17-3 advantage and with that fourteen-point cushion, Beaumont's men ran everything. Twice more they came within feet of crossing the All Blacks' line and suddenly the supporters, swaying in their precarious tree perches, began to realise they were witnessing history being made. Some had even shinned up the temporary scaffolding of the television tower and not all were able to hold on till the end. The great All Blacks' coach Fred Allen was later to describe the North's performance as, 'The best display I've ever seen against an All Blacks' side anywhere in the world.'

As the final minutes ticked away and the pace dropped, Stuart Wilson was able to catch the North's backs napping to run in a face-saving try, converted by Richard, and New Zealand could at least console themselves with the knowledge they had crossed their opponents' line. They seemed prepared to settle for a 17-9 scoreline but Beaumont and his men hadn't finished with them yet.

Billy exhorted his forwards to one last effort and they responded by actually pushing New Zealand off their own ball at a scrum near their line. Smith snatched the ball but instead of trying to score himself, executed a perfect scissors with Alan Old, leaving the fly half clear to run in the last try un-opposed. It was a thrilling finale to an unforgettable game and there was no prouder man in Yorkshire than Fylde's Billy Beaumont when the whistle sounded to confirm a Northern victory by 21 points to 9.

The home changing room soon resembled Wembley after a cup final Saturday. There was no shortage of drinking and smoking material as the celebrations got under way amidst the mud and the steam. Even the All Blacks joined in the fun. Mourie was generous in his praise, conceding that his side had been out-thought and out-fought and concluding that defeat in those circumstances was no disgrace. The warmth of his message remains one of Billy's happiest rugby memories. It crowned the victory more completely than if all fifteen players had been chosen to play for England, and the after-match banquet was equally euphoric.

But Mourie was a canny skipper as well as a magnanimous one. He saw his main objective as winning international matches so instead of brooding on the result, he had resolved to match the plotting and scheming that had preceded this game. Twickenham and England were a fortnight away and victory there was now all that mattered.

As it happened, the England selectors were to throw him a lifeline. The team they chose was a good one, leaning heavily on the North. But it had one glaring omission – Alan Old was not asked to repeat his tactical role at fly half, but instead the young Leicester player, Les Cusworth, was brought in to partner Smith and win a first (and very nearly, last) cap. Cusworth was a good player full of positive ideas and superb at providing a quick ball for his backs. That was the way Leicester, under top coach Chalky White, played. And they were far and away England's best club side. But at that stage of his career, Cusworth was not a great kicker and the

England hierarchy had decreed that the national side would play the same tactical game as the North had done at Otley. From the start, such a concept was doomed to failure.

Cusworth had a wretched afternoon. Smith's service was slower than usual and with a firm ground, Mourie, Mexted and Stewart were fully a yard faster breaking from the New Zealand scrum. The fly half never had a chance to settle down. Afterwards, in an interview with *Rugby World*'s David Norrie, Beaumont was to defend the selectors' choice of team, saying instead, 'We played badly that day. People have said the selection was wrong. They're wrong: the selection was right. They picked fifteen players who were capable of winning for England that day, but unfortunately, we did not produce the goods.'

Later, he would amend that judgement, conceding that Cusworth should not have been asked to play so unnatural a game. But the lesson was that he had confidence in Rogers and his team of fellow selectors and was as prepared to support them in public as in private. It was commendably loyal, especially in the context of previous mistakes and misinformation emanating from on high.

Alan Old wasn't the only distinguished absentee at Twickenham. Peter Dixon, nearing the end of a great career but still one of the most creative back row forwards in the world, was also left out. Mike Rafter came in to act as a terrier on the flank but the tactic didn't work. New Zealand had regained their composure by then and made precious few mistakes. Even so, they were lucky to win.

Richard Wilson had regained the form which so cruelly deserted him at Otley and his two penalty goals, coupled with a fine try from lock John Fleming, gave the All Blacks a ten-point lead before England had settled to their game. New Zealand are always loathe to concede an initiative once established, and though Beaumont's team grafted effectively enough to monopolise possession in the second half, Dusty Hare's three penalty goals never looked like more than compensation. The final score of 10-9 suggests a close struggle – but it wasn't. The crowd seemed muted even though they could see their team controlled most of the play; somehow, they didn't seem to believe in an England victory.

Beaumont was bitterly disappointed by the result but he faced the press willingly and, with what we all took to be a piece of bravado, announced that he had seen enough from his team to convince him a Triple Crown was in order for England, possibly even a Grand Slam in the International Championship. No one actually laughed outright but there were a few sniggers and one or two pencils hovered uncertainly over their notebooks.

It was Billy, of course, who had the last and the loudest laugh.

12

1980: PHOENIX FROM THE ASHES

The mantle of favouritism sat uneasily on Irish shoulders. They were renowned for upsetting the odds but unused to making them. Yet most of the rugby press and all of the leading bookmakers gave them the edge, despite the fact that their opening match would be in the graveyard of past Irish hopes, Twickenham. We should have known better.

Ireland's credentials for their unaccustomed role had been drafted in Australia the previous summer. Not only had they won both test matches but while doing so had the temerity to drop the 1979 Player of the Year, Tony Ward, in favour of the tall, slightly-built Ollie Campbell of Old Belvedere. Campbell's only previous appearance in Irish colours had been as far back as 1976, also against Australia and his strength lay (apparently exclusively) in an uncanny ability to kick goals from any corner of the field. Ward could do that too as well as run explosively at and through the opposition. His defence was not in question and if there was a major technical deficiency in his play it was simply that his passing was cramped and perhaps lacked real snap. But still, by any rational judgement, Ward was at the beginning of 1980 a far more complete player than Campbell and, crucially, more experienced.

The Ward-Campbell debate should logically have been settled at the Irish trial in January but Ward was nursing damaged knee ligaments and it was decided he should not be risked. So instead, Campbell's opponent in the Possibles side (the Blues) was the

London Irish stand-off, Hugh Condon, partnered by the excellent John Robbie.

Any last, lingering doubts – despite Ward's absence – were settled as far as the selectors were concerned in that match. Campbell kicked four conversions and two penalties as well as running in three tries – twenty-six points. The man from Dublin was clearly a 'winner', a quality always easier to recognise than to define. I sensed then that he could go all the way and wrote in my International Championship preview in *Rugby World*: '. . . And in Ollie Campbell, the fly half who seems likely to keep Tony Ward out of the home internationals this time, they (Ireland) have perhaps the key player. I've a sneaking suspicion that it will be the Irish who finish on top for the first time since 1973, and that Ollie Campbell will become a household word on this side of the Irish Sea.'

I was right in my second prediction – Campbell scored a Championship record forty-six points. But I was wrong in the first. Ireland eventually finished joint second alongside Wales. As for England, the best I could say about their prospects was: 'England's problem will be one of confidence. A win against Ireland could set them on their way, but there must be a serious question mark about their ability to sustain a challenge through four tough matches. They invariably produce one outstanding result each season but that suggests a team better equipped as spoilers than as champions. We shall see.'

What I had failed to appreciate was that the North West tour of South Africa and Rhodesia, the North's win over the All Blacks and, going back still further, England's unbeaten tour of the Far East, had bred a confidence and resilience in the English outfit that was as potent as the qualities that carried them to their last Grand Slam in 1956. The second parallel was that in 1956 they had been captained by Eric Evans, a players' player who would run through brick walls for his country and expected others to do likewise. And in 1980, they were captained by a man, Billy Beaumont, cast from precisely the same mould.

The New Zealand result had thrown a smokescreen over England's real strengths because the selectors had made some obvious howlers, and paid the penalty. The after-match press conference when Billy had thrown his hat into the ring on behalf of England had been too readily dismissed as brave optimism. On his behalf, I recorded the following:

'All this talk about a Wales/France/Ireland carve up of the honours brings a wry smile to the face of England captain Billy Beaumont. The burly Lancastrian is convinced that 1980 will prove to be England's year – at worst, the Triple Crown. The evidence is less compelling.'

But the evidence was to mount swiftly as first the Irish, then the French and most notably of all, the Welsh, were dismissed in quick succession. Ireland had chosen the bulk of the forwards who had triumphed in Australia in 1979, most notably the back row trio of Fergus Slattery of Blackrock, the captain, John O'Driscoll of London Irish, and the old campaigner at Number 8, Willie Duggan. Moss Keane had Jim Glennan of Skerries to partner him in the second row, and he was a newcomer. But the front row was the same mix of toughness and experience: Phil Orr of Old Wesley, Ciaran Fitzgerald of St Mary's College and Gerry McLoughlin of Shannon.

At half back, Campbell was partnered by Colin Patterson of Instonians. The pair had played together in the Trial and quickly struck up an understanding. If there was a weak link it was perhaps the selection of the Broughton Park and Lancashire full back, Kevin O'Brien, in place of the tried and tested Rodney O'Donnell of St Mary's College. O'Brien owed his selection to a string of excellent performances for Lancashire and the North (the Beaumont connection again), but in the event, he was to prove a bitter disappointment.

The England side was almost precisely the one Billy would have picked. Dusty Hare was at full back. The elegant Nick Preston of Richmond joined Bond in the centre and they were flanked by Carleton and Slemen. At half-back, Steve Smith was asked to renew his successful partnership wih John Horton of Bath, which meant there was no place for Alan Old. After his performance for the North against the All Blacks, Old seemed the obvious choice to play outside half in the Championship, but somehow, the selectors had developed a blind spot where the Yorkshireman was concerned. As for Old's successor, Les Cusworth of Leicester, he was made the scapegoat for England's lamentable performance against New Zealand at Twickenham and left out of the squad altogether. That black mark against the selectors has since been redeemed and Cusworth was given another chance to prove his ability in 1981.

At forward, the England team reflected the strength of rugby in the North generally and Lancashire in particular. Uttley and Neary were the flankers with John Scott of Cardiff at Number 8; Nigel Horton narrowly won the vote over Maurice Colclough to partner Beaumont in the second row; Phil Blakeway of Gloucester came in at tight head prop to complete a formidable front row, with Cotton on the looseh ead and Wheeler at hooker. This was not quite the best fifteen England would field in the season but it was only a point or two off it.

With so much at stake, and with Ireland established as favourites, England made a desultory start. The Irish back row covered every inch of Twickenham in the opening minutes as they sought to harry England into mistakes, but, significantly, Beaumont's men were immovable in the set pieces: solid in the scrum, dominating in the line-out. Even so, England hardly deserved the early lead which Hare's penalty gave them.

Ireland took it in their stride, or at least, Campbell did. Three times England transgressed and three times he punished them by casually stroking over penalties, none of them within easy range. A less resilient side might have dropped their heads at that point, but Billy was right when he described this England team as 'built on guts and character'. They simply knuckled down to the task, setting the priority on eliminating silly technical offences. It was clear that Campbell was in the mood and form to kick goals from anywhere.

As England tightened their game so Ireland began to feel the pressure of that powerful scrummaging machine. Blakeway's phenomenal strength had him lifting the experienced Phil Orr clean out of the scrum, at times giving Wheeler the chance to strike fast and first against the less experienced Fitzgerald. It meant slow ball for Ireland when they did win it and the occasional morale-boosting strike against the head for England. The psychological advantages were all with England as the first half drew to a close.

With ten minutes left for play, Smith showed just how much he had improved since his last period in England colours. The South African tour had made him a good yard faster and his eye for an opening was acute. A ruck formed close to the Irish line and as England won the ball, Smith gathered and powered his way over. Hare converted to make the score 9-9, and minutes later, England went ahead when Smith put in a teasing diagonal kick towards O'Brien. The full back misread the flight and attempted to fly hack the ball to safety. He missed and Mike Slemen collected the perfect bounce to run in and score unopposed. Again Hare converted and England turned 15-9 ahead at the interval.

Billy didn't say much at half time. He didn't need

to. Every England player was giving his all and the captain simply went round each in turn reinforcing their growing confidence by patting them on the back and letting them see the commitment written all over his face. England responded by setting up camp in the Irish half straight from the half-time whistle and it was inevitable that the pressure would bring its reward with another score.

But just as it seemed Ireland must be swamped, tragedy struck. Tony Bond, whose fierce tackling had kept the Irish backs muted all afternoon, was caught in a double tackle and suffered a terrible injury. His leg was broken and he was carried off the field on a stretcher, a sponge clenched between his teeth as he fought off the waves of pain. It was a stunning blow not just for Bond and England but for the Lions too because the powerhouse Sale centre looked made for the hard grounds of South Africa.

'It's ironic,' he recalls, 'that I received my Lions availability slip a couple of hours before I broke my leg. My father handed it to me as I arrived at Twickenham and I never got the chance to fill it in. As for the injury, it was a pure accident. I went to tackle Alistair McKibbin and when I got hold of him I was tackled from the side by Slattery and Neary. That caused me to twist at a time when all my weight was on my left leg. The studs stayed firmly stuck in the ground, my body twisted round and I ended up with what they call a spiral fracture. I was upset because I felt I was having my best game in an England jersey. I felt really confident.'

Billy was as stunned by the accident as his players but he knew that any relaxation now by any of them could prove fatal, and the first man he spoke to after the incident was Clive Woodward of Leicester, Bond's replacement. His words were simple and to the point. '*You* are playing for England now. Play your heart out.' Woodward did just that and the smooth pattern of England's play was barely disrupted.

Dusty Hare consolidated England's lead with another penalty and with the Irish beginning to flag, Beaumont's men seemed home and dry. It was left to John Scott of Cardiff to put the icing on the cake with a try near the end, his first for England. From a scrum ten metres out from the Irish line, the giant Number 8 broke with the ball and barged his way through a forest of green shirts. Once more Hare was on target with his kick and the final score read, England 24, Ireland 9. It had been a totally convincing win, summed up, perhaps, in the key statistics which showed England had won the conclusive line-outs 25-15, the rucks 18-12 and the mauls – Ireland's traditional strength – 11-7.

'We're off and running!' was Billy's happy post-match comment.

13

1980: SILENCING THE COCKEREL

The most important lesson Beaumont had learned
from the Ireland match was that with proper
preparation, seemingly insurmountable hurdles
quickly diminish in size. There was no disputing the
height of the obstacle that faced them in Paris, yet no
one in the team doubted it could be overcome. To a
large extent, Beaumont himself was instrumental in
creating the positive mood that carried England
across the Channel with all guns blazing.

France sent out a hotch-potch of a side, one that
could be either brilliant or abysmal – such is the
French way. Discarding Paco in favour of Dintrans at
hooker, for example, seemed illogical, yet Dintrans
was to play a storming game. On the other hand, with
a clear need for fresh blood in the second row,
Duhard and Maleig replacing Haget and Marchal
looked a lively combination. They ended up as lambs
to the slaughter against Beaumont and his powerful
new partner Maurice Colclough. Carpentier was an
optimistic choice to take on the fast-improving John
Scott at Number 8, while the selection of Salas to
oppose Blakeway at loose head prop was simply
eccentric. Salas was a useful lock, nothing more.
Blakeway was the toughest tight head in the business.

But many had reservations about the England side,
too, especially behind the scrum. The loss of Bond in
the centre was a severe blow to Billy's tactical plans.
Preston had done well enough against the Irish and
was just the kind of nippy, top-of-the-ground runner
needed to create openings against a ponderous

defence. But the choice of Woodward as his partner was more of a gamble.

The Leicester man had proved an adequate substitute for Bond in his first international but, like Preston, he was essentially an attacking and rather unpredictable player. He lacked experience at this level and Paris was renowned as a graveyard for those winning their first full cap. By far the biggest worry in the England camp was how the midfield would perform if they found themselves having to defend a slender lead. No one could knock the opposition over like Bond.

So this was to be the match that would really test the character of the new England, and they were given no time to ease themselves gently into the match. France went ahead after just two minutes, Bertranne making a powerful run in the centre before passing inside to his scrum half, Gallion, who in turn slipped the ball inside to the flying John Pierre Rives. The French captain crossed the line near the corner flag, too far out to give Caussade a comfortable first kick at goal. He missed it but had he converted the try the French might have concluded it was to be their day and acted accordingly. Many a fine team has been put to the sword by the sheer weight of Gallic optimism, but Beaumont kept calm, and so did his team, while Dusty Hare set out to prove that four points means nothing when he has his kicking boots on. The Leicester full back was on target with his very first attempt, a penalty, just five minutes later, and to many observers England appeared to be having significantly the better of the forward exchanges. Even the three points they conceded when Cotton was penalised for foul play and Caussade duly kicked the three points soon afterwards, failed to dent English morale. Not a single head dropped.

A steady diet of possession turned into a veritable flood midway through the half. Beaumont and Colclough took full possession of the line-outs while

Blakeway tortured his opposite number, Salas, in the front row. The forward drive was impressive and in the loose, England seemed quicker and more alert. So a score became inevitable and it was forward pressure coupled with lightning fast passing that saw England notch their crucial first try.

A ruck inside the French 22 gave England quick and tidy possession. Preston took a neat pass on the burst and Bustaffa and Gallion were left floundering as the Richmond centre flew through the gap. Hare couldn't quite work a miracle with his conversion attempt from far out on the angle, but at 7-7 England were looking good value and getting stronger by the minute. A second try quickly followed.

This time it was Scott who initiated the move, picking up and breaking from a scrum with Colclough and Beaumont at his shoulder. As the Number 8 was tackled he moved the ball on and Smith was alert enough to create an overlap for Carleton to sprint clear for the line, crossing about ten yards in from touch. Hare was again off target with the difficult conversion.

England suffered their first serious setback just before half-time when Uttley emerged from a pile-up bruised and bleeding and was forced to leave the field for treatment. The cut required a number of stitches, but in the ten minutes he was off the pitch, England actually increased their lead, thanks to the opportunism of fly half John Horton. Collecting a loose ball in the French half, Horton made space to send over a beautiful drop goal. As the whistle went to end the half, England were 14-7 to the good and the French hadn't even managed a serious counter attack.

Uttley was still absent when the second half began and just when it seemed England could no longer risk playing with fourteen men and Beaumont seemed set to call for a replacement, Horton struck again. This second drop goal was even better than the first and stretched the England lead to an impressive ten points. No sooner had the score-board proclaimed the fact than the craggy features of Uttley emerged from the tunnel, head bandaged and bloodstained. England were back at full strength. For the next quarter of an hour, Beaumont urged his side to keep the game tight and they responded by drawing the French forwards into a remorseless series of rucks and mauls with Smith and Horton using any scraps of possession to kick the French further back into their own half.

The tactic was an obvious one but it had its disadvantages. England had established such a moral superiority that they had become used to dictating the play, especially in the midfield. Once they sat back to defend, the French became more adventurous. Fast passing movements from whatever possession they could glean began to stretch England's defence and when, fifteen minutes from the end, Averous broke down the left wing, he found only Carleton between him and the England line. The Orrell man moved in to tackle but was stunned by a pulsating hand off from the Frenchman as he dived for the corner. Caussade landed an excellent conversion and at 14-17, France were very much back in the game.

The defensive qualities of Preston and Woodward were now tested to the full. Time and again the French tried to attack down the middle and each time the slightly built England centres cut them down. The back row trio of Neary, Scott and Uttley were equally deadly in support and gradually, the attacking waves lost impetus.

France threw in everything in those dying minutes but even the baying of the crowd and the tireless example of their blond captain, Rives, couldn't find a way through the England line. Referee Clive Norling of Wales blew for the end of the game and suddenly, England were half way to a Grand Slam.

The English supporters who had made the annual

pilgrimage to Paris more in hope than expectation were so thrilled by the victory that there were still hundreds of them inside the ground an hour after the game had finished. Many were to be encountered later in various stages of celebration as the England party let their hair down and went on the town. Of all the matches in the international calendar, the one in Paris is the most fraternal off the field. The French may seem uncompromising on the pitch but off it, they are perfect hosts and excursions to the Moulin Rouge and other nightspots are *de rigeur*.

Billy's recollections of the Saturday night are understandably hazy. 'I recall arriving back at the hotel with Maurice (Colclough) and Dusty (Hare),' he remembered, 'just as the rest of the boys were preparing to leave for the airport the next morning. And somewhere along the line, we had a late dinner – or was it early breakfast? – in some bistro or another. But as for the rest . . . It was one of the best nights of my life.'

England had shown character in Paris, a point conceded without reservation in the press. But they had also shown great skill. The pack had developed into a quite awesome unit, mobile as well as strong, and almost telepathic in its understanding. Rives, the French captain, had recognised their exceptional quality even before the match in Paris.

Two days before the teams met he told David Frost of the *Guardian*: 'I am worried by the England forwards. They have so much experience. We have always known there are a lot of Lions dotted around your country, but it seems to me this is the first time you have allowed so many of them to play together in the same team. Cotton, Wheeler, Uttley, Neary, Beaumont – that must be a difficult pack of forwards to play against.'

In voicing his disquiet, Rives must have been equally aware of just how lousy a hand of cards the French selectors had dealt to him. Blakeway had made enough of a mess of the experienced Phil Orr in the Irish game, so to feed him the untried Salas was plain suicidal. The unfortunate prop was never picked for France again.

To add to Beaumont's joy, Ireland had knocked off Scotland 22-15 in Dublin to remove a second contender for the Triple Crown so it was already clear, halfway through the campaign, that the England v Wales match at Twickenham would decide the destination of the Championship. That fact alone was to have an immense bearing on the spirit in which the game would be played. Not since the sixties had England and Wales met with so much at stake, and the press played up the importance of the impending clash for all it was worth. No memory remains as vivid in Billy's mind as that bloody encounter. But his bitterness remains directed at the media, not his opponents. 'Their attitude,' he says passionately, 'was unforgivable.'

Even today the rights and wrongs in the matter remain blurred enough to arouse passionate debate. But there was no mistaking the victim, Paul Ringer of Llanelli, whose sending off by Irish referee David Burnett for a late tackle on John Horton had Twickenham in uproar.

14

1980: THE MATCH THAT DIED OF SHAME

It would be no exaggeration to say the match at Twickenham effectively ended Paul Ringer's career. His play, always robust and passionately committed, lost its cutting edge when he returned after an eight week suspension. He played on for Llanelli in a desultory sort of way and was even given a vote of confidence by his team mate and skipper, Ray Gravell, by being appointed vice captain for the 1981 season. But with further international honours denied him and the attention of press and public focused on him each time he ran out on to a rugby pitch, he concluded the point of playing on had gone and he announced his retirement from the game shortly before the first Welsh squad for the International Championship in 1981 was announced.

So what happened to turn a 'villain' into a martyr and sour the showpiece game of international rugby in Britain? There is no doubt a section of the press created a mood of attrition two weeks before the game and Beaumont is right to castigate the journalists concerned for stirring the pot. But he misses a point or two in confining his criticism to the media.

In the first place, the Welsh team that began the 1980 campaign was not the dazzling, all-running outfit the public had feasted on in the seventies. It was a little long in the tooth in key areas – even Ringer was thirty – and there was a disturbing toughness about its play which had its genesis in Paris, not Twickenham. In that game, which the

Welsh won 18-9, scoring four tries in the process, there were allegations of foul play which soured the traditionally convivial banquet afterwards.

The French have never seemed the most saintly nation when it comes to robust forward exchanges but, on this occasion, they were victims not villains. The main controversy centred around Ringer, whose 'careless' footwork was alleged to have caused head injuries to Paco and Rives. The allegations were widely reported in the press and many lofty scribes demanded that Ringer be left out of the Welsh team, guilty or not. That, not unnaturally, offended Welsh sensibilities: Ringer was, at that time, an outstanding and speedy loose forward and Wales could ill afford to do without his presence. So he was picked to play against England and it was *then* that the media knives began to come out.

The *Daily Mirror* fired the opening salvo, not via its regular rugby correspondent but through a reporter who alleged a fued was brewing between Wales' Graham Price and England's Fran Cotton. Once the ball began rolling, it quickly gathered momentum and the match took on all kinds of nationalistic connotations quite alien to the spirit of rugby. Billy Beaumont recalls a squad training session on the Friday before the game when he had to go around his team cooling them down rather than psyching them up for the coming confrontation.

Twickenham was, as usual, packed to the rafters, but there was an air of expectancy among the crowd quite foreign to a normal match. Trouble was anticipated and it arrived within a minute of the opening whistle. A line-out was the signal for a near free-for-all with elbows and fists flying as the players came to grips. In the RFU committee box officials of both teams shifted uncomfortably in their seats.

David Burnett, an affable Irishman with a laid-back sense of humour and a reputation for letting a game flow, was the referee chosen to take charge. He surprised himself by the amount of whistling he had to do in the opening minutes. This was clearly going to be a match requiring firm control and he was soon calling the captains together to issue a general warning. Beaumont and his opposite number, Jeff Squire, were told that the next player to transgress would be off – no questions, no arguments. Both men returned to pass the message on to their team mates.

The scrums still came together as if propelled by battering rams and the line-outs were contested with frightening intensity, but boots and fists were kept firmly under control. It seemed as though Burnett's message had got through. But then, out of a clear blue sky, came Ringer.

England fly half John Horton fielded a loose ball and quickly banged it into touch. It was on its way long before Ringer's high tackle came in and the England player went down as if he had been pole-axed. Burnett ran across. Penalty to England, he decreed, marching orders for Ringer. The sad Welshman, hands on hips, trudged silently from the pitch. Hare kicked the penalty and those three points were to prove crucial at the end of a game which Wales had many subsequent chances to win.

After Ringer's dismissal, the mood softened noticeably. It was as if the steam had been taken out of the game and passions expended in one incident. And ironically enough, once Wales found themselves with fourteen men, they began to play high quality rugby and it was only England's indomitable spirit that enabled them to come back and win the game.

After Hare had put England into the lead, Wales knuckled down to their task, reorganising the scrum to such effect that they were able to contain the drive and even disrupt the England put-in with some clever wheeling. It was just such a tactic that led to a vital score.

England had been forced back almost to their own line and when a loose maul degenerated into a pile-up with no prospect of the ball emerging, Burnett ordered a set scrum. It was England's put-in and Wheeler seemed to win the strike. Suddenly, Wales wheeled the scrummage, throwing England off balance and the ball squirted out of the side. Squire pounced and was over the line for a shock try.

Stung by the reverse, Beaumont exhorted his men on to greater effort and gradually they worked their way into solid attacking positions in the Welsh half. But there was a lack of sparkle about their back play and the Welsh cover defence proved well capable of repulsing each pedestrian attack. Half time was beckoning when England suffered another setback.

Roger Uttley was trapped on the ground as the Welsh mounted an old fashioned foot-rush and he received a boot square in the face. The blow split his face, spreading his nose and covering everyone in blood. The damage was severe enough for the luckless Uttley to have to leave the field and the tension mounted once again. Geoff Wheel was adjudged the culprit but most agreed it had been an accident. So half time came with England 4-3 behind against fourteen men and needing to play with greater poise and direction if they were to maintain their proud record.

Wales seemed to thrive on mere scraps of possession and twenty minutes into the second half they were still looking the likely winners. Had fly half Gareth Davies, centre Steve Fenwick and lock Allan Martin been on form with their place kicking, England would have buried long before the end, but somehow that second score eluded them and it was England who regained the initiative with fifteen minutes to go.

Yet another penalty was signalled, this time in England's favour and Dusty Hare dutifully collected the three points. It was now just a question of hanging on. But still the Welsh attacked and with a little over two minutes to go, Elgan Rees made the vital break and hurled himself over in the corner for a spectacular try. It was a score they richly deserved and it came because in England's desperation to bang every ball deep into Welsh territory, Steve Smith had allowed the Welsh hooker, Allan Phillips, to get too close and charge the kick down.

That should have been that, but incredibly, England were to get another bite at the cherry. From the kick off, the ball was scrambled into touch and Beaumont called for a two man line-out. Scott won the ball, palmed to Smith who threw a low pass out which Beaumont, of all people, collected around about his ankles. He found support on his right shoulder in the form of Paul Dodge and the England centre ran at the Welsh defence to set up a ruck. As the ball remained stubbornly trapped, Welsh scrum half Terry Holmes went over the top in his anxiety and frustration and England were awarded a penalty. Everything now depended on Dusty Hare.

Twickenham was as silent as the tomb as the full back ran up to take the kick. It soared high and clear between the posts and to everyone's amazement, England had won. There was no time for Wales to set up another attack and the whistle was the signal for thousands of jubilant supporters to descend on the pitch.

After the game, Billy was summoned like royalty to wave to the crowd from the committee box. It was a moving and emotional moment for the England captain as he surveyed the swaying throng of chanting supporters. The three major hurdles had been negotiated and the least England could expect from a momentous season was a share of the International Championship.

But before thoughts of the future were allowed to crowd in, something had to be done about the present. The press were waiting, epithets sharpened for an explanation of the violence. What they got was a muted, diplomatic – perhaps restrained – performance from the England captain and the chairman of the selectors. The message was that the game had been an aberration and could never be repeated. And Billy had the same message for the Welsh players when he went into their dressing room soon after the final whistle had sounded to shake hands and commiserate with Jeff Squire. The Welsh captain agreed and there was no hint of the aggression that had shocked the rugby world left in either camp. The after-match banquet was as convivial as ever although like actors after a first night, the players and officials of both teams dreaded the notices in the newspapers the next day. They were not disappointed.

15

1980: GRAND SLAM!

Fleet Street gorged itself on the 'Battle of Twickenham'. Every paper had a news story to accompany the match report and some were moved to editorialise. It made sickening reading for Beaumont. As England captain, he was expected to speak on behalf of all the players and, being the honest, forthright character he is, there was no attempt to absolve his team from their portion of the blame. The fact that he faced the issue so squarely had a reassuring effect on both the media and the administrators; it helped show the way forward and shift the emphasis from recrimination to prevention. Rugby could ill afford so bad a press again.

The immediate effect in Wales was to still all the natural fire and enthusiasm that normally accompanies their play at international level. Against Scotland they played with a caution bordering on the timid. Yet they still showed enough skills to come away on the right side of a 17-6 scoreline. Later, Jeff Squire admitted that his players had performed as if in handcuffs.

The automatic suspension of Ringer ruled him out of the rest of the campaign. Indeed, he didn't reappear at international level — and only then on a modest, domestic scale — until March, in the Heineken Sevens in Amsterdam as part of the Steep Holm side. In the meantime, a small industry had grown up around him. 'Ringer is innocent' tee shirts began to flower and he was even immortalised in song by the admirable Max Boyce. Not everyone thought the martyr portrayal in good taste, but at the end of the day, words and pictures, however humourous, would mean nothing. His glory days were over.

With their third win tucked safely away, England now stood poised for a tilt at the Grand Slam. History and recent form suggested they would come away from Murrayfield victorious and bookmakers were quoting odds as prohibitive as 7-1 on for England, 3-1 against for Scotland. But as Ireland had proved at the start of the championship, the mantle of favouritism can weigh heavily on the shoulders, and England had a long month to kill before the crucial game. Meanwhile, the press stoked up interest almost daily.

One piece of news that didn't make the papers was the appointment of Billy Beaumont as Lion's captain. He had been given the news at the post match banquet following the Wales game by manager Syd Millar. He was shocked, flattered, excited . . . and sworn to secrecy! It must have been frustrating to be forced to sit on such a thrilling bit of news. Only Hilary shared the secret.

Finally, the big day dawned, and Edinburgh was a madhouse. The pubs and hotels, always crowded at international time, were literally bulging with would-be celebrants on the morning of the match. It seemed as though half England had crossed the border. Princes Street experienced pedestrian traffic jams greater than even the Welsh had managed to achieve on their traditional sorties. I remember parking my car somewhere in the city centre and setting out on the long, leisurely walk to the ground. But instead of strolling, I found myself impelled along the streets on a cloud of beer and cheap whisky. All routes led west to Murrayfield (which is situated on the outskirts of the city) and pity any stragglers who couldn't keep up the pace. As kick off time drew nearer the scene resembled Pamplona at the running of the bulls fiesta.

Inside the ground, 75,000 people stood, sat or

staggered as they contemplated the feast that awaited them. I found myself wedged into a corner of the bulging press box next to David Duckham, a man who had experienced triumphs galore on that lush Murrayfield turf but now fretted and scowled with worry for England at the prospect of what lay ahead. The game was just fifteen minutes old when the worry lines were turned into smiles.

Clive Woodward, collecting the ball in midfield outside the Scots 22, jinked inside his man and then raced for the corner before straightening up to draw the defence and sending out a perfect pass for John Carleton. The winger had enough room to touch the ball down in a spot which gave full back Dusty Hare a reasonable shot at goal and his conversion put England 6-0 ahead. No sooner had the crowd settled down again after the excitement than Woodward was weaving another bit of magic, this time creating a chance for Mike Slemen to go over in the other corner. Again Hare was on target, 12-0 to England. When Carleton scored his second and England's third try within half an hour following clever work on the blindside of the scrum by Number 8 Scott and scrum half Steve Smith, it seemed England had taken the match out of range. Sixteen points was a huge margin especially with the backs looking so sharp and the forwards cleaning up in tight and loose.

Andy Irvine finally got Scotland on to the scoreboard in the first half with a penalty which thudded against an upright but went over. Just before half time, Hare landed a convincing penalty to bring England up to 19-3 at the break and, straight after the restart, Irvine kicked another three points to make it 19-6. The match was now poised. Any further score for England was likely to be decisive while Scotland, in their occasional attacking bursts, seemed to suggest that one try would lead to others. It was England who seized the initiative.

England won yet another line-out, this time

through a decisive two-handed catch by Roger Uttley, and he set in motion a move that involved a dozen English players and ended with Steve Smith touching down the try. Hare couldn't convert this time but 23-6 seemed suitably decisive. What changed the picture was a sudden sharpening of Scottish forward play. They began to win some quick, clean ball instead of living solely off scraps, and the backs found they had time and room to expand their attacking options.

Jim Renwick, a clever, elusive centre, ghosted his way through the centre and found ready support from lock Alan Tomes. It was Tomes, in fact, who had helped to inspire the Scottish resurgence up front and now he was on hand to make an even more tangible contribution, a try. Irvine converted – 23-12. Sadly for Scotland, though, their enthusiasm led also to carelessness and England were awarded another penalty which Hare duly converted. And then England hammered another nail into the coffin when a high kick by Paul Dodge in the centre bounced unkindly for the Scottish full back and the eager Carleton accepted the present to run in his third try, the first hat-trick by an Englishman since 1924.

But still the coffin lid refused to stay shut. Rutherford, the fly half, made a beautiful break which so wrong footed the English defence that he was able to sprint through unopposed to touch down for a try between the posts. Irvine converted, and as the match entered the final ten minutes, Scotland continued to attack at a bewildering pace. Keith Robertson, Andy Irvine and David Johnston each made telling runs which would surely have resulted in tries had not the England defence been so resolute. Billy, exhausted by his own efforts but so full of adrenalin that he continued to scamper about the field like a two year old, inspired his team through example. Each Scottish wave was repulsed, the minutes ticked away and finally, the French referee,

111

Pierre Bonnet, put the whistle to his lips to signal the end of a thrilling, red-blooded match. As Billy later put it, 'I was aching to hear the final whistle and suddenly it went. We were champions. We had done the lot!'

He remembers too, being surrounded by ecstatic England players and supporters, but particularly by the three players with whom he had shared so many of the bad times that now seemed a million light years away – Peter Wheeler, Fran Cotton and Tony Neary, playing in his forty-third match for England, a record that still stands. Wheeler and Cotton chaired their captain off the field.

Back in the dressing room the ritual champagne was broken open. Players, reserves, selectors, all revelled in the pride and excitement of the occasion. Bruises were ignored, past disappointments forgotten. Billy slipped away to thank Irvine's team for a magnificent game and when he returned, the party was in full swing. But before the celebrations could take over completely, there were other duties still to perform. The first was a speech which embraced all those who had worked so single-mindedly to make the moment possible, and the second was a brief but moving presentation of an inscribed silver tankard to Tony Neary in recognition of his personal achievement in setting a new caps record. It was typical of Beaumont's thoughtfulness that he should have spent half the morning of the match scouring Edinburgh for a silversmith who would engrave the tankard in time. It illustrates perfectly the qualities that made him so universally respected as a captain, the kind of captain who could lead men into the jaws of hell without question or protest. Neary was visibly moved. No one knew then that he had played his last and most memorable game for England. A higher note on which to finish could hardly be imagined.

Next began the round of television and press

interviews which Billy had come to find not only easy but thoroughly enjoyable. His relaxed and affable manner in front of the microphone had already endeared him to the vast proportion of rugby followers and was a pointer to what would follow when his playing days came finally, and prematurely, to end. He was never a 'natural' but as in everything he attempted he worked and learned and achieved a level of excellence. Finally, there was the after dinner banquet and his first chance to discuss the possible composition of the Lions touring party with the manager, Syd Millar. The names were to be announced the following Monday though selection would take place on the Sunday afternoon. Millar made it clear there were question marks still, particularly over the composition of the front row. Was Cotton the right choice at loose head prop, or had he, as England chairman of selectors Budge Rogers concluded, lost some of his appetite for the game? Beaumont was emphatic that Cotton was as committed as ever – his skill remained unquestioned.

It is significant that Beaumont was not only consulted but got his way. Cotton was indeed in the party of thirty-eight announced later. Perhaps the game against Scotland had tipped the balance? Certainly it ensured the inclusion of Jim Renwick at centre and the workhorse of the second row, Alan Tomes. There would be no place for Geoff Wheel, Beaumont's friendly protagonist, but allowing for the enforced absentees – either through personal, business or injury reasons – the selectors dealt him a very strong hand.

The choice of Syd Millar as manager and Noel Murphy as coach also had a positive, encouraging ring. Murphy was the senior coach in the British Isles at the time and had worked miracles with the Irish side on their successful tour of Australia. He was also one of the best flank forwards that country has ever produced – perhaps the finest. Millar, meanwhile, was the brilliantly successful coach of the 1974 Lions in South Africa and the ablest of administrators. Criticism of the trio that led the party could be confined to only one point – they were all forwards and experience has shown that is not the ideal combination. Yet it had worked in 1974 and that date remains the focus of excellence in British rugby. Lions teams are judged as either better or worse than then. Beaumont's might have been better. But no one would ever know for sure because what happened was unprecedented. Beaumont was about to embark on the most searching examination of his life.

16

1980: WOUNDED PRIDE – THE LIONS IN SOUTH AFRICA

No tour in international history has been as ill-starred as the one Billy Beaumont led to South Africa in 1980. Not only did a vastly superior group of players squander one winning chance after another in the test matches, but they were so decimated by injuries that almost one third of the original party was replaced during the two-month safari. 'I spent more time welcoming and seeing people off at the airport than a travel courier,' is Billy's wry recollection.

The jinx actually struck before the Lions left London and it was one of their most experienced players, Andy Irvine, who was fored to pull out. Irvine had been playing for a Scots invitation side in the Cathay Pacific Hong Kong sevens the week prior to departure and, in the final, he tweaked a hamstring. It was the kind of injury that niggles if it is not treated properly, and the only certain cure was rest and heat treatment. Neither could be properly effective on a tour which involved hundreds of miles of travelling. Irvine was replaced and asked to prepare himself to fly out later as a replacement should he be needed. He was – about eight times over!

Because of the controversial, in other words political, nature of the tour, it was decided to forgo the traditional training and general get together period on the South coast prior to departure. Instead, the Lions would assemble in London on the eve of departure to forstall any possibility of demonstrations from opposition groups. This clandestine procedure allied to Irvine's sudden withdrawal led almost directly to Wales' Elgan Rees becoming a Lions member for the second, and equally surprising, time in his career.

'Harry', as he was nicknamed on the 1977 tour, was at Heathrow airport with the Welsh squad waiting to depart for a tour of North America. He never boarded the plane. Instead, the Lions' management sent an urgent message to the Welsh officials requesting the winger's services for a couple of months. Hours later, he found himself heading south with Beaumont's party while his colleagues flew west.

Billy had misgivings about this unorthodox piece of selection. He admired Rees but would have preferred it if the more experienced England player Peter Squires had been called up, even though it might have been a week before he could join the tour. As it happened, Rees played six times and scored three tries although he never made the test team, and indeed, was one of many serious injury victims. But in a sense the decision underlined the positive, no-nonsense approach of the Millar-Murphy management team. They knew what they wanted and when they wanted it and the players came to respect their forthright attitude. Billy tells an amusing story which further illustrates the point.

At the dinner prior to departure some of the tourists ordered wine with their meal. But, according to Billy, somehow the bill received a low priority rating when it became time to settle accounts. As there were no ready volunteers to settle up, Millar decreed that the tallest man in the room would pay and then do his own dectective work to recoup the cost. The tallest happened to be the Wales' lock Allan Martin and it was several weeks before 'Panther' collected his dues. It is ironical that Millar, of all people, should have proved such a strong, able manager. He was the classic example of 'poacher turned gamekeeper', a Lion whose exploits as hellraiser and fireman in 1966 have passed into rugby legend.

The sudden and secret departure successfully headed off all demonstrations and the Lions arrived in Johannesburg on a Sunday morning to prepare for the first game against Eastern Province in Port Elizabeth with barely a voice raised in protest. Indeed, Billy is emphatic that from the time he was confirmed as captain until the time they returned, not a single letter or telegram denouncing the tour was received by him or his family. It's a fact, but a curious one considering just how sensitive an issue sporting contacts with South Africa had become and considering that this was the first major breach in a boycott of that country since the last All Blacks' visit in 1976.

The loss of Irvine had been a blow, but at the time, no one would have considered it an ill omen. Yet in the first week the Lions were in South Africa, two more key players were sidelined before a ball had been kicked in anger. David Richards, the first choice centre from Wales who was also an outstanding performer at fly half, learned of the sudden death of his father and was immediately flown home. Then Ollie Campbell, whose goalkicking ability was considered crucial, strained a hamstring while practising and was forced to take a prolonged rest. Other players, including Billy, suffered painful blisters and grass burns from the unexpectedly hard grounds and so the first 'Saturday' side that took the field on May 10 was by no means the one Beaumont would originally have selected. Only the pack was complete as a unit and even that was to be fatally disrupted.

All pundits had agreed that while the general composition of the party was sound, it had one glaring weakness. There was no tearaway flanker in the Fergus Slattery-Tony Neary mould; both had been forced through business reasons to stay at home and the man chosen to fill the vital role, Stuart Lane of Cardiff and Wales, was something of an unknown factor.

Just how unknown was cruelly demonstrated when the Welshman tore knee ligaments just fifty-one seconds into the first match and had to be stretchered off the field. He never played on tour again and the Lions were ultimately forced to adapt their tactics to accommodate the style of their other flankers, O'Driscoll, Squire, Tucker, and later, Gareth Williams.

But that wasn't the end of the story. Campbell's counterpart at fly half, Gareth Davies, was another casualty of the opening game, injuring his shoulder so badly that he would be ruled out of contention for a month. And Phil Blakeway, the strongman of the front row, aggravated a rib injury and, like Lane, was unable to take any further part in the tour. So within a matter of days, the second replacement was winging his way out to the high veldt: Ian Stephens, the Bridgend loose head prop who had some – but strictly limited – experience as a tight head. He joined Gareth Williams, who had been 'hijacked' in North America as he toured with Wales, and the one bright spot was the news that Richards would be able to rejoin his colleagues once funeral arrangements for his father had been completed.

So after one match, the Lions were in disarray although they had won handily enough, 28-16, and scored their first tries of the tour. These early, quite unexpected, blows drew on Beaumont's qualities as a leader in a way he had hardly anticipated. And the fact that he came through them with so much credit was to be a crucial factor in restoring morale. He had seen it all before, he told his players, and even the worst crises could be overcome. But what followed was unprecedented and finally taxed the party beyond the limits of endurance. The injuries were, in essence, the story of the tour.

Above: The end of the affair. Lancashire coach Des Seabrook *(right)* and physiotherapist Kevin Murphy, escort a concussed Beaumont from the pitch during the County Championship final at Moseley in January, 1982. *(Bob Thomas)*

Below: At the Palace. Beaumont and wife Hilary pose for the cameras outside Buckingham Palace, 1982, after receiving his OBE. *(Colorsport)*

We are the champions! A mud-spattered Beaumont holds aloft the
Thorn County Championship trophy in February, 1980. Colin Fisher *(left)*
and Fran Cotton are the shoulder bearers.
(Colorsport)

Above: When will the jinx end? South African referee lends a sympathetic ear to the Lions' captain as medical men and team mates tend to injured centre David Richards in the match against Transvaal. *(Colorsport)*

Below: No threat to Botham. The British Lions' captain sweeps inelegantly to leg in a one-day cricket match during the 1980 South African tour. *(Colorsport)*

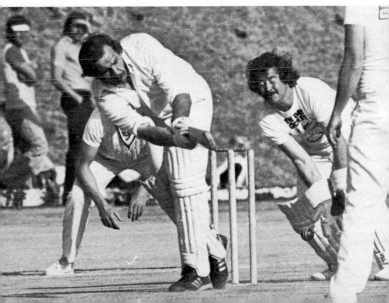

Above: Holding the line. Beaumont stands firm amidst a spate of terrier-like tackles from the Irish in the international at Twickenham in 1976. *(E. D. Lacey)*

Below: Two gentlemen of rugby. Beaumont and France's captain, Jean Pierre Rives, exchange handshakes in Paris after England's thrilling 17-13 at Parc des Princes in February, 1980. *(Colorsport)*

Above: Charge of the heavy brigade! Beaumont leads the rush with Roger Uttley and Fran Cotton in support at Murrayfield in March, 1980. Scotland's diminutive centre Jim Renwick bravely stands his ground. *(Colorsport)*

Below: Grand Slam! Beaumont is chaired off the field at Murrayfield by jubilant team mates and supporters after England had clinched their first international clean sweep for 25 years. *(Colorsport)*

Above: The end of a dream. Lions' captain Beaumont is still stunned as he and South African skipper Morne du Plessis give a television interview minutes after the decisive third test at Port Elizabeth. *(Colorsport)*

Below: The best in the business? The 1980 Lions' management team of Beaumont *(captain)*, Syd Millar *(manager)* and Noel Murphy *(coach)*. *(Colorsport)*

Down and out at Bloemfontein. Beaumont is the man at the bottom of the pile with his second row colleague Maurice Colclough *(with headband)* 'nursing' a pair of Springboks. *(Colorsport)*

Above: Lions' prop Fran Cotton is helped from the field clutching his chest with a suspected heart attack. The diagnosis proved faulty, but Cotton never played international rugby again. *(Bob Thomas)*

Below: The author displays a specially commissioned pottery sculpture of Beaumont at the 1980 Player of the Year lunch in London. *(Colorsport)*

The tour itinerary had been designed to ease the Lions in gently for the first fortnight. Eastern Province should have been easy meat – that they weren't was the fault of the tourists. And it seemed to many of the huge press party assembled that a convincing win against their next opponents, the South African Rugby Association Invitation XV, was in every sense crucial. Once Natal were encountered in the third match in Durban, the opposition would get stronger and stronger, and the travel, long, tiring and ultimately bewildering.

Vivian Jenkins has been on Lions tours both as a player – vice captain in South Africa in 1934 – and reporter – chief rugby correspondent of the *Sunday Times*. He knows all the perils and all the pitfalls and is emphatic when he says, 'A tour of South Africa is the hardest rugby assignment of them all.' The vast distances that must be travelled on an itinerary that criss-crosses the country present problems in themselves. But more significant are the altitude changes, from the dry, dusty air of Johannesburg on the high veldt, to the damp, almost soporific breezes of the Cape coast. Form can vary alarmingly in such conditions and it was for this reason that Beaumont was concerned to pack as much experience as possible into the touring party. The players injured in that opening game were simply unlucky, but the danger of 'silly' injuries occuring by over-zealous training or foolhardy dives on the concrete-like ground, was real and ever present. Remembering the 'torture' session he had undergone in New Zealand under John Dawes, Beaumont had insisted there would be no repeat for his players, yet for a while it looked as though coach Noel Murphy was overdoing things when he packed seven sessions into the first four days. The redeeming feature was that each session was so carefully planned and filled with such variety that the players never had time to get bored. Two hours seemed to fly past. The tiredness would come later.

119

East London, where the SARA game would be held, was just up the coast from Port Elizabeth. The Association's representative side had been so unsuccessful up to that point in the season that they had even conceded eighty points to a North West Transvaal under twenty-five team. On paper, it looked a gift of a game.

But even gifts sometimes have a sting in the tail. This one was that SARA (the Panthers, as they were known in South Africa) had stiffened their side by the inclusion of eight white players, including Thys Stofberg, one time favourite to captain the test team from Number 8 or flanker. The racial connotations cut both ways. The match would be historic because it was the first time the Lions would face a truly multi-racial side — a fact welcomed by Beaumont and his players. But at that point in South Africa's development, there were no Cape Coloured players remotely in the same class as their white counterparts, and therefore, the 'white contingent' could make this a very tough game indeed. The fact that the Panthers would be a scratch side would work in the Lions' favour to some extent, but players with something to prove are players to be feared.

It was agreed that Beaumont should sit this one out and the captaincy passed to the experienced Welshman, Derek Quinnell. The return of David Richards was welcomed by all, especially as his ability to play fly half gave the Lions an extra option. England's Clive Woodward was given a chance to show that he was not just a superbly skilled runner but no mean performer with the boot; his sixteen points (three penalties, two conversions and a dropped goal) were a revelation to his colleagues and were the foundation of the Lions' 28-6 win. Even so, the victory was not convincing and there were ominous signs that South Africa's long enforced isolation had left their referees with a somewhat loose interpretation of the laws. Quinnell spent a

120

considerable proportion of his time asking Mr Smith-Belton to clarify this or that infringement as Panthers rose from the line-outs as if propelled by mechanical hoists. In the end, he gave up the unequal struggle and simply shrugged his shoulders in resignation. Of greater concern was the obvious decline of the Lions' tight head prop, Phil Blakeway. He had been packing at an eccentric angle all afternoon and his pace around the field – never of firecracker proportions – gradually slowed almost to a halt. He came off at the end of the third period and it was obvious his damaged ribs were more damaged still. Perhaps the only positive note was struck when Elgan Rees scored his second successive try of the tour, showing something of his old, blistering pace. Perhaps his call-up had not been so 'crazy' after all.

Now came the first real 'test' of the tour. Natal had the kind of pack that had a Springbok look to it and it was clearly time for the Lions to put their very strongest combination into the field. That meant Beaumont taking charge again, his blisters having been reduced to manageable proportions if not entirely healed, and the young Scotsman, John Beattie, was given a chance to prove that he and not Derek Quinnell was the Lions' answer at Number 8. Ollie Campbell was paired for the first time with scrum half Terry Holmes, and this too looked like a test match combination. Campbell's rival, Gareth Davies, was back in some sort of training but his shoulder was still strapped and a three-week layoff was the most optimistic prediction for his time off the field.

Just before the game, the verdict on Blakeway was finally delivered. His ribs would not heal in time for him to take any useful part in the tour and, with great reluctance, the management decided to send for their second replacement, Ian Stephens. Both Lane and Blakeway would be flown back to England immediately after the first test.

121

The game itself answered one or two significant questions. The pack was blending together well. Beaumont had a tight, constructive game in the second row and Allan Martin, looking unusually fit and lean, jumped with authority in the key position in the middle of the line. Cotton, Wheeler and Price looked unstoppable in the front row. For the first time, the entire fifteen men who started the match for Lions finished it – but that was merely a statistic. Campbell only did so because of a grim, though stubborn determination. His hamstring had tweaked more than once during the afternoon and by the evening he was in sufficient pain to suggest he might become another first test casualty. Yet again, Millar, Murphy and Beaumont were forced to hold a crisis meeting. Now they needed cover at fly half and the one man who seemed to have the class to slot straight into the side was Ireland's forgotten hero, Tony Ward. The decision to send for him spoke volumes for the democracy of the triumvirate: Murphy, the coach, was no fan of Ward's, considering him talented but far too selfish. Still, he readily conceded the point. Ward was asked to fly out.

The fourth match took the Lions inland to Potchefstroom for an even tougher fixture, against a South African Invitation XV. The Lions took a calculated gamble in weakening the pack to give key players a rest, and it worked – but only just. The final score was 22-19, another cliffhanger, and it turned out to be the game that will live in the memory after even the tests have been forgotten. Contained within it, a perfect rugby cameo, was a try that will rank with the greatest. It began with fly half David Richards in the Lions' own half and ended with Mike Slemen crossing the Invitation XV's line under the posts. In the meantime, eleven Lions were directly involved in a move which saw the tourists handle an incredible thirty-three times. The sequence was timed at one minute forty-five seconds, and every precious moment of it was captured on video film. It has already become a request classic when the BBC are compiling sports programmes. Carwyn James, the legendary Welsh coach who masterminded the Lions 1971 series win in New Zealand, later wrote: 'The try, which will of course always be remembered, was similar in style to one scored by J.P.R. Williams for the Barbarians against the All Blacks in 1973 or the try scored by Alan Richards for Llanelli against Dawie de Villiers' Springboks in 1970 when the ball passed through twenty-three pairs of hands and three rucks. [But] perhaps the try hid the fact that it was only on a couple of other occasions the Lions spun the ball.' There amidst the euphoria was perspective. Not cold water, because James was as thrilled as any of the spectators by the magic of the moment. But he saw what others did not – the Lions were brittle behind the scrum in a way that other touring sides had not been.

The Lions' test side was slow in taking shape. Beaumont was anxious. Against Orange Free State in Bloemfontein, yet another half back combination would be tried, this time pairing Richards with Terry Holmes, his Welsh international colleague. It was by no means a success. Holmes was harrassed throughout the match despite the dominance of the Lions pack, and later, he damaged his knee ligaments badly enough to join the list of casualties whose tour was prematurely at an end. The Lions won 21-17.

There was just one more game before the first test and it was to be played to a background of violent events off the field which made front page news both at home and abroad. At Bethel, a small black township, protests against the government's second class education policy for blacks had become ever more vocal. Finally, they erupted in violence after schoolchildren staged a protest strike. The demonstrations were put down in a savage manner.

News of the disturbance reached the Lions party

and caused much disquiet among the players. But to some extent Beaumont and his colleagues were insulated from the scene. They kept their counsel publicly while the press party, pressurised no doubt by editors in London wanting a 'Lions link' to an international story, began to file stories of discontent. There were calls among anti-apartheid groups in England for the party to be recalled, most vocally through the only black member of the Sports Council, Mr Paul Stephenson. His remarks were treated seriously, though any linking of the Lions presence with the unrest was strenuously denied at home and abroad. Even so, Mr Stephenson was assured that the Lions would return if the manager, Syd Millar, requested it. He did not and there the matter was allowed to rest and simmer until the middle of June, when Ian Todd of the *Sun* wrote a front page story claiming fifty per cent of the touring party were so disillusioned by what they had seen in South Africa that they wanted to return home. Not only was this one also denied, but it was taken seriously enough by Millar and Beaumont for the players to be polled on their feelings. As it turned out, not one player voted to return. None of which is to say that consciences were not under siege. They were. Beaumont himself agonised over what he saw and read in the papers. But he, and others, remained convinced that what they were doing was in the best interests of black and coloured players in particular and sport in general. He holds that view as firmly today.

The final, warm-up match before the first test on the troubled Cape was against a SARA Invitation XV at the historic Stellenbosch University ground. The Lions were to win 15-9 but pay a price so heavy that Billy Beaumont maintains their morale never fully recovered. They lost Fran Cotton, the most popular member of the touring party, with what appeared at the time, and for a day or so afterwards, as a heart attack.

Cotton had been suffering from inflamed varicose veins on the tour and was far from fully fit when he played against Natal. His recovery had been worryingly slow, but Murphy, anxious to get him back in action before the crucial first test, decided to chance Cotton in the SARA game. Later, Murphy would suffer agonies, wondering whether he had sent his player if not to his death, at least into premature retirement. It worries him still.

Carwyn James and Chris Rea who covered the tour for BBC radio, maintained at the time that Cotton looked ill from the very start of the game. He was given a rugged time by Le Roux, playing flat out – and not always fairly – for a test place. Finally, Cotton admitted to Alan Tomes at a line-out that he was suffering from chest pains, and the Scot's response was immediate and unequivocal. 'Get off the pitch – now!' Cotton accepted the advice and the pictures of him being led from the pitch clutching his heart remain a poignant image of the unlucky tour. The first diagnosis was that Cotton had indeed suffered a mild heart attack and he was rushed to hospital for more tests.

On the pitch, the violence continued unabated, inflamed by some dreadful refereeing – easily the worst on the tour so far. The scrums came together like battering rams, and in the line-outs, it was all niggle and the occasional flying fist. Both Millar and Beaumont were universal in their condemnation of the South African play and the after-match banquet was a tense affair. Fortunately, Beaumont was not there. He had a pressing though far less palatable engagement, at the hospital where Cotton lay bewildered and distressed.

Billy stayed at Stellenbosch hospital while Quinnell gave a biting after-dinner speech, and when he satisfied himself that Cotton was not in any immediate danger, he put through a telephone call to Fran's wife, Pat, in England. He remembers it like this:

'I phoned from my hotel room, doing my best to put her mind at ease. "Hello, Pat. It's Bill phoning from Cape Town." "Oh, my God!" she exclaimed. "What's happened to Fran? Is he all right?" I gave her a watered-down version of the story, told her not to worry and promised to ring her again in the morning with further news.'

Cotton was transferred the next day to Groote Schuur Hospital, famous as the hospital where Dr Christiaan Barnard performed his pioneering heart transplant operations. Cotton could not have been in better hands. And there was soon encouraging news: it had not been a heart attack but an inflammation of the muscle tissue around his heart caused by a virus. He was in no danger though he was unlikely to play rugby again. Cotton remembers thinking, 'Here I am, thousands of miles from home, and I've hardly seen my young daughter.' The incident made headlines all over the world.

With the Cotton incident it seemed the Lions must surely have at last run out of bad luck. But they hadn't. There were more injuries to follow – one almost fatal – and in between there was the disaster of the first test.

126

17

1980: WINNING BATTLES, LOSING THE WAR

Beaumont's first sight of the fabled Newlands ground at Cape Town filled him with horror. The pitch was a disgrace, bare, bumpy and rutted. A modest rainstorm would have been enough to turn it into a quagmire, and that in turn could make the result a lottery. On the other hand, in its present state it could provide serious handling problems for the new full back, Rodney O'Donnell, unless his catching and positioning were impeccable. A high kick bouncing on the 22 could end anywhere. On balance, rain might be the better option.

All speculation was banished the day before the game with the arrival of 'The Cape Doctor' a brisk, south-westerly wind like the French Mistral that signals dry weather and drives the fog and the smog away from the city. So the Lions could expect an aerial bombardment after all and Naas Botha, the 22-year-old wunderkind of South African rugby, was the ideal offensive weapon.

Botha was a phenomenon. In fifty-three first class games he had scored 661 points, a staggering average of twelve and a half points per match. He could kick goals from any angle and any range, but his skills as an out half had yet to be tested at top level. Ironically though, it was as a jinking running fly half that he won schoolboy international honours. It was much later that he changed his style to safe handling and big kicking.

The men, outside Botha, were largely an unknown quantity to the Lions management – all except the winger, Germishuys, who was earmarked as Tony Ward's 'Aunt Sally'. Syd Millar remembered Germishuys from his days as coach to the 1974 Lions and he convinced Beaumont and his colleagues that the winger had a habit of spilling anything delivered to him from aloft. He was to be peppered with high balls all afternoon on this dubious premise and was not only to catch them all, but return them with interest.

To win the first six games with relative comfort – though not all the scores suggest that – convinced Billy that the first test match was well within the Lions' compass as long as they adhered to a tactical plan based on forward domination and made few mistakes. He had seen nothing to frighten him in the early matches. Murphy and Millar were of like mind and while it was worrying to go into so important a game with a fly half who was desperately short of match practice, at least Tony Ward was experienced and of proven class at the highest level. As it turned out, Ward was very nearly a match winner, scoring a record eighteen points through five penalties and a dropped goal.

With Fran Cotton out of action the front row of the pack looked, on paper at least, less formidable than the Lions would have liked. Yet Clive Williams had acquitted himself well enough in the fourth game of the tour against a South African Invitation XV in an all-Welsh front row. Allan Philips was the hooker, Graham Price the tight head prop and the test match hooker, Peter Wheeler, had had no problems adapting to his new partner in the following game, against Orange Free State, the team coached by the South African national coach, Nelie Smith. As one of the opposing props in that game would also play in the tests, le Roux, Price's adversary, the Lions had a fair measure of what might lie ahead. The back row had been reshaped to accommodate both O'Driscoll and Squire with Quinnell at Number 8. That made it potentially slower than Beaumont would have liked but at the same time, meant they had the ideal men in possession to operate the rolling maul. This was a ploy the South Africans were unfamiliar with and despite its shortcomings, it gave the Lions an edge up front that they were able to sustain throughout.

Right from the kick off, the Springboks charged into the fray, pumped high by their own adrenalin and lifted still further by a baying crowd witnessing international rugby at the very highest level for the first time in many years. This frantic, all-action running unsettled the Lions. An early, confident score for the tourists might have changed the whole course of the tour, instead, within the first minutes of the game they had made one of the multitude of ghastly mistakes that would haunt them for the rest of their careers.

Tony Ward, hero and villain of the Lions, hoisted a speculative kick towards touch which Springbok full back Gysie Pienaar swallowed with glee. He ran on, chipped the ball over the advancing Mike Slemen's head and collected the rebound before cutting inside Ward's incoming tackle. Rob Louw, the fast, skilful flanker who was to be a constant thorn in the Lions' side, came up to drive his way over the try line with a trio of Lions trying desperately to hold him up.

Beaumont was philosophical about the early blow. The bounce had been fortunate for Pienaar. There was only one way to treat the incident – forget it, stay calm and work methodically back into the match. The forwards took his soothing words to heart and the Springboks began to take a terrible pounding up front. With neutral French referee, M. Palmade, keeping a tight rein on line-out illegalities, the Lions found themselves with three kickable penalties in the first half. Ward kicked them all, and he needed to. Beaumont's advice had gone unheeded by full back O'Donnell who continued to scamper after the ball like a scalded cat. He cost the lions both the second and third tries.

The first came after the centre, Willie du Plessis, chased a teasing high kick from Botha. Remembering the state of the ground and the inevitable high bounce, O'Donnell should have gone for a clean catch at all costs. Instead, he let the ball go to ground and it squirted past him like a pip from a melon. Before he could turn, du Plessis had gathered and raced joyfully over the line to score. Botha converted.

The second try had bad luck written on it. The Lions were desperately cumbersome in trying to gather and clear the ball near their own line and, finally, it popped up off O'Donnell's boot and into the arms of the ferociously strong lock, Moaner van Heerden. He bulldozed his way through some woeful tackling and Botha was again on target with the conversion. So the Lions were 16-9 at half time and no one could quite believe it.

As if to make immediate amends for their lapses, the Lions increased their tempo after the break and put the Springboks in all sorts of trouble. Ward kicked his fourth penalty within minutes of the restart and then, after a sustained spell of pressure on the South African line, prop Graham Price grabbed a loose ball and became a wedge for O'Driscoll and the other forwards to drive over for a try. So now the scores were level and the Lions were cock a hoop. Ward added to their joy moments afterwards when he chipped a neat drop goal with his left foot after jinking inside Louw's challenge. At 19-16, it seemed the Lions were home and dry.

But after doing so much to give the Lions a winning chance, Ward then handed the initiative back to the Springboks with a woeful kick infield which Germishuys caught to launch a fast counter attack. Pienaar, Mordt, Louw, Pienaar again, and finally the instigator of the move, Germishuys, all handled before the winger dived over in the corner. Botha kicked a good conversion and now the Lions trailed 22-19. Ward made up partially for his lapse by then kicking his fifth successful penalty of the match and his eighteenth point in all – a new record for a Lion against South Africa. It levelled the scores and by now, most Lions supporters would have settled for that. The match was almost two minutes into injury time when Serfontein delivered the coup de grace.

The Springboks – rarely for them – won a line-out on the Lions' 10 metre line and spun the ball out to Smith with Mordt coming into the line and then moving it on to Willie du Plessis. Germishuys carried on the move before releasing it to Mordt once more and the winger was brought down by Patterson's tackle five yards from the line. The rampant Springboks were up on the breakdown in a flash. Willie and Morne du Plessis drove on, supported quickly by their pack, while the Lions tried desperately to hold up the drive. Finally, the ball popped clear to Louw who had the simplest of tasks to put Serfontein over. It was bitter, heart-chilling stuff for Beaumont and his men.

Self-inflicted wounds are always the hardest to heal and they hurt like no other. Billy knew they had simply blown it and it made him both angry and sad. His own play had been formidable, peeling off from the line-out to collect the accurate tap backs of his partner Maurice Colclough, and driving hard into the Springbok cover until they were bruised and weak. All the forwards did well but the backs let them down. Poor, superstitious Rodney O'Donnell felt the most wretched of all. He could not be consoled and he began back-tracking over his day to see which particular routine he had missed to earn such outrageous bad luck.

O'Donnell's superstitions have become the stuff of legend. In his book about the tour, co-authored by BBC Radio commentator, Chris Rea, Carwyn James wrote:

'O'Donnell's superstitions were a minor sensation

131

in South Africa. He refuses to walk on lines and so must zig zag across the hotel foyers. He must be last on to the bus and last into the changing room. He cannot go on to the field three times. When Ireland played France he had to go on the field for inspection, and then the French asked him to go on for a photograph. This was a terrible problem and O'Donnell refused until Noel Murphy undertook full responsibility for whatever happened to him in the game that day. He has great trouble going to bed because he must not touch the bottom sheet or the top sheet with one part of his body. He throws off the cover and jumps into bed, landing on his back so that all his body touches the bed. At home, he has to walk out of his door backwards. He has so many superstitions that he cannot always remember them all.'

In the wake of the first test, Beaumont saw it as his primary duty to build morale once more for the sterner battles that lay ahead. Almost every waking day for the Lions now seemed to contain its quota of good news and bad news, and usually, the bad news was more emphatic. Carleton had been substituted at Newlands by Ray Gravell, a move that reduced the Lions' attacking options, though perhaps marginally, stiffened their defence. How long Carleton would be out of action was anyone's guess. The former Orrell schoolmaster (he had given up his job to go on the tour) was one of the toughest, most determined characters in the side. He was quite likely to buck the odds and declare himself ready before the second test at Bloemfontein a fortnight hence. But for Mike Slemen, the most talented all-round footballer in the party, the South African adventure was quite definitely over.

Before the match in Cape Town, Slemen had told Beaumont that his domestic problems had become so pressing that an early return home was essential.

Slemen's wife was expecting their second child. It was a difficult pregnancy, high blood pressure having forced his wife to remain in hospital for periods of treatment, while their son, Michael, had begun to pine for his father in a way no words of comfort or condolence could cure. Billy, sensitive as ever, agreed that Slemen's duty was to his family first and so, within hours of the conclusion of the first test, the Lions' potential ace in the backs was on his way home. The good news came when a telephone call to Andy Irvine broke the news that the Scottish skipper was fit and willing to join the party. It gave the Lions three outstanding goalkickers, four once Davies' fitness had been established, and should have been the turning of the tide. It was not.

There were good victories in provincial games against the South African Country Districts (27-7) at Windhoek; Transvaal in Johannesburg, 32-12; and Eastern Transvaal (21-15) at the industrial town of Springs. But in that final match before the second test, the Lions lost their first choice scrum half, Terry Holmes, and the injury was serious enough to rule him out of the rest of the tour.

The match in which the Lions lost Holmes was also the match in which South African refereeing lost its last vestige of credibility. Mr Johanus Steenkamp made so many eccentric, or just plain bad, decisions that he earned the dubious accolade of 'the worst referee I have seen or played against'. The critic was Billy Beaumont, and nothing in the intervening time has caused him to revise the opinion.

There were lighter moments in the tour, particularly off the field, where Billy 'bagged' a kudu on a big game hunting expedition at Windhoek. The single shot required to kill the beast was marksman-class. But once the thrill of the hunt was over, Billy felt physically sick because of what he had done. The kudu is a form of antelope, bigger and less elegant but no less appealing for all that. He vowed there and

133

then that he would never attempt to kill an animal again. It was an attitude which left his hosts bemused but one that will perhaps be better appreciated in a country like Britain.

The airport round continued, of course. Slemen was seen off, Dodge was welcomed. Soon Robbie of Ireland would come to replace Holmes; later still, Steve Smith. By the end of the tour the replacements would number eight and the walking wounded at various stages, perhaps twice that. Ironically, this was the first tour which had its own travelling Doctor, Jack Matthews, the former Wales centre who could hardly have anticipated such a busy 'holiday'.

But as the second test approached, the trials and tribulations – including more press stories about 'disillusionment' – were forgotten. The task at hand became paramount, and the Lions chose a team that should have blasted the over-confident Springboks into kingdom come. It read like this: Full back: Andy Irvine; Wings: Bruce Hay and John Carleton (duly recovered, as he had promised); Centres: Ray Gravell and Clive Woodward; Fly half: Gareth Davies; Scrum half: Colin Patterson; Props: Graham Price, Clive Williams; Hooker: Peter Wheeler; Locks: Billy Beaumont, Maurice Colclough; Flankers: John O'Driscoll, Jeff Squire; Number 8: Derek Quinnell.

A packed house at Bloemfontein saw the Lions lose an early lead, regain it, lose it again – and trail for the rest of the afternoon. The first try came in almost exactly the same way as the opening score at Newlands, Irvine being the culprit on this occasion with a poor kick which Germishuys fielded to start a thrilling move. The ball moved to Morne du Plessis, then to Rob Louw, next to Willie du Plessis and finally, it was Louw who went over in the corner. Botha couldn't convert.

The Lions hit back through O'Driscoll, fast becoming the key loose forward of the tour. As Serfontein fumbled a clever little kick ahead by

Patterson, O'Driscoll snatched up the loose ball and dived over. Gareth Davies was on target with the conversion – 6-4. Botha took the Springboks back into the lead when Price went into a ruck with boots flying and a penalty was awarded against the tourists – 6-7. Next, Stofberg scored after an incident so controversial that Beaumont maintains it cost the Lions the test series. Many neutral observers agree.

Mordt, the Springbok winger, was tackled outside the Lions 22 and to most eyes, the ball seemed to go to ground. Under the laws he could no longer play it until he had first released it and regained his feet. But instead, he got up with the ball and ran on before putting Stofberg over. Beaumont was angry enough to write later that 'Palmade's one serious mistake of the match cost us the series'. The reverse so upset the Lions, that it was no surprise when they slipped further behind when Botha followed his successful conversion with a penalty kick. And Davies' penalty just before half time to make the score 9-16 seemed nothing more than dubious consolation.

Still, again the Lions pack were cleaning up everything in sight, and the second half was only just under way when they clawed back six points through penalties by Davies and Irvine which brought them within touching distance of the Boks at 15-16. Tragedy struck soon after. Davies went down with a serious knee injury and Campbell came on to substitute. The Lions had been awarded a penalty, forty yards out, but in a straight enough line to suggest the Irishman would gobble it up without concern. Billy threw him the ball. Campbell ran up, kicked and the ball hooked wide of the posts. 'In retrospect, I suppose I should have given the ball to Andy (Irvine),' Billy said later. 'But he wasn't kicking that well at the time and I thought Ollie would get it.' It was the last chance for the Lions. After that, mistakes multiplied and the Springboks took an iron grip on the game.

A high kick from Pienaar landed in no-man's land and Germishuys beat Carleton to the ball to touch down for a try — 15-20. Next, Pienaar himself scored a try after captain Morne du Plessis had set up the ball after a Lions mid-field breakdown — 15-24. The conversion by Botha was perhaps the best of his life, certainly it put the final nail in the Lions' coffin. At 15-26, there was no way back. But just before the end, Ray Gravell showed alertness and determination to squeeze his way over for an unconverted try to make the final score 19-26 and leave the Lions with the galling prospect of trying to win the final two tests just to square the series.

Beaumont himself was a casualty as the weary players trudged off the field. His knee had swollen up to twice its size and the anxious management found themselves faced with the prospect of losing their influential skipper. Fortunately, a South African doctor who examined the knee persuaded Billy to accept a radical treatment. He inserted a hypodermic needle and painstakingly, drained off more than a third of a pint of blood. By next morning it was stiff but back to normal size. Under physiotherapy, it might have taken two months to heal.

There was a profound air of depression about the Lions party as they trooped wearily to the plane that would carry them 600 miles north from Bloemfontein to Johannesburg. Four of the most important selections at the beginning of the tour, Gareth Davies, Terry Holmes, Fran Cotton and David Richards, were not on board. Instead they were en route to London, casualties of a sequence of accidents unprecedented in sport. Adding to the air of gloom were the South African press reports of the test which suggested the Springboks were only one step away from establishing themselves as true world champions. This eulogy brought a wry smile to the face of captain Beaumont and his colleagues in the pack. Only they knew just how comprehensively the Boks had been beaten up front.

There was no respite in Johannesburg. The Lions' opponents, the Junior Springboks, were a crack selection on paper, and to emphasise just how seriously they were taking the game, the Juniors went into hiding until kick off time. This 'professional' approach didn't go down too well with the touring management, but they kept their council and the players resolved to do all their talking on the field. Billy, his knee responding well, decided a match on the sidelines would get him in just the right frame of mind to resume the battle. So the captaincy passed to Jeff Squire and Allan Martin was drafted into the second row.

The score at 17-6 to the Lions was flattering. This was one of the least convincing of their performances and had the Juniors taken even half the many chances they created they would have run up a cricket score. As it was, the Lions had a solid performance from debutant Paul Dodge to thank for creating enough scoring chances to enable them to stay ahead. Renwick dropped a goal early in the game and then Irvine, Rees and Dodge scored tries. Irvine was not an original selection at full back and the fact that he was able to gain much-needed match practice in that key position was the result of a tragic, near-fatal accident to the unlucky O'Donnell.

The Lions' full back seemed intent on rehabilitating himself in this game following his disastrous display at Bloemfontein. His positioning was more confident, his catching secure and his tackling brave and effective. It was this bravery that cost him dear. Danie Gerber, the stocky Springbok centre, tried to burst through the middle and O'Donnell tackled him head on. The collision was frightening and no one in the ground was surprised when only Gerber got to his feet. Luckily for O'Donnell, his fellow Irishman, John O'Driscoll, was also playing, and as O'Driscoll happens to be a doctor as well, treatment was instant and decisive. One look convinced O'Driscoll that the neck was dislocated and any movement by unskilled hands could cause paralysis, or even be fatal. Expert medical help was soon on the scene and with infinite care and patience, O'Donnell was eased into the correct position and taken away on a stretcher. In hospital he was put in a brace and the specialists concluded that while he would probably never play rugby again, neither would he suffer any permanent damage. Bearing in mind the enthusiasm of first aid men in South Africa and New Zealand, it would be no exaggeration to say O'Donnell owes his life to O'Driscoll.

The injury naturally cast a pall over the Lions' celebrations of victory and, to add to the gloom, Phil Orr had badly gashed his thigh during the match, which kept him out for three weeks. But on the bright side, the form of Irvine at full back had given hope for the third test and the experiment of playing Clive Woodward on the wing seemed worth repeating. In fact, for the game against Northern Transvaal the Lions fielded their full test side bar one, John Robbie playing while the test berth was to go to Colin Patterson. The Northern Transvaal game was to provide the Lions with one of their best wins of the tour, a great morale booster before the Port Elizabeth clash.

In the aftermath of the Northern Transvaal victory, Springbok hopes of winning the Port Elizabeth test evaporated. Suddenly the newspapers were full of gloom and doom and David Norrie – who had flown out to cover the finale for *Rugby World* – reported in his first despatch that not a single pundit he spoke to believed South Africa could pull it off. Billy Beaumont was confident too, especially when the rain swept in over Port Elizabeth and the temperature dropped alarmingly. It had already been decided before the game that the confidence of the

138

backs was at such a low ebb that it would be a forward battle from start to finish, and in the prevailing conditions, that was a tactic he relished.

Beaumont lost the toss but to his surprise, Morne du Plessis elected to play into the driving rain and wind. This put the onus on the Lions getting off to a flying start, something they had signally failed to do up to that point. This time, it was different. A late tackle gave Ollie Campbell a chance to kick a penalty and as it sailed over it seemed to mark the change of fortune Billy had been praying for. Even a good reply by Naas Botha failed to dent Lions optimism because a splendid piece of opportunism by Bruce Hay on the wing (picking up a loose clearance by Serfontein) had also given them the only try of the half and an interval lead of 7-3 was pleasing enough.

Immediately after the restart, Botha dropped a neat goal to narrow the gap to one point and Billy realised it was time to drive his team on to greater effort. The lead was pathetic reward for so much possession: one correspondent estimated that the Lions had had at least 70 per cent of the play, winning line-outs, rucks and mauls. Beaumont and Colclough were working brilliantly in harness and the only criticism that could be levelled at the forwards was that they tended to overdo the rolling maul and released the ball to their backs too slowly and too infrequently. Once Campbell had restored confidence with a second penalty, it seemed the match was over bar the shouting. No one could have anticipated the heartbreak that was to come.

Clive Woodward had proved an adept winger in two earlier games. He was quick and elusive and his tackling had looked secure. But it was a position in which he was, to all intents and purposes, a novice and it was ultimately his inexperience that cost the Lions the match. Botha put a low ball over Woodward's head and it practically died on the greasy surface. Woodward turned and deciding discretion was the better part of valour, sidefooted the ball into touch. An experienced winger would have belted it into kingdom come – and he certainly wouldn't have then turned his back to position himself for the line-out. Germishuys grabbed the ball before a ball boy could touch it – and therefore make it 'dead' – threw immediately to Pienaar, accepted the return and sprinted over unopposed in the corner. Woodward held his head in his hands in despair. The scores were level and the victory the Lions had done so much to achieve had again eluded them.

Beaumont recalls watching the incident from thirty yards away on the other side of the field in horrified slow motion. He could see exactly what was going to happen and was totally powerless to prevent it. A draw was simply not good enough. The Springboks felt the same. Such luck could not be squandered and Botha approached the 'impossible' conversion from far out in the mud as if his very life depended upon it. Until this point, his place kicking had been indifferent. Now it was majestic. The wet ball took off and sailed between the posts to make the score Springboks 12, British Lions 10.

Even at the fifty-ninth minute of the eleventh hour, the Lions had a chance to salvage the game. A penalty was awarded in their favour and Campbell was asked to repeat the attempt he had had in the second test to turn the game. That time he had hooked it, now it sailed straight as an arrow – but his alignment was wrong and it flew past the post. All that was left was the agony of the final whistle. And agony it certainly was.

At the after-match banquet, Dr Danie Craven, usually the most diplomatic of men, told his audience he knew exactly how the Lions felt. 'It is not easy,' he intoned, 'to take a hiding.' The remarks were not well received! Morne du Plessis was more conciliatory, but nothing could disguise the bitter statistics which showed the Lions as losers of the series by a minimum of three tests to none. Even more galling was the memory of the chances they had again squandered – Dodge and Irvine spilling passes with the line in range and Patterson taking on the Springbok defence with a two man overlap outside him. The rest of the tour was a salvage operation.

Faced with the chilling prospect of being the only Lions captain in modern history to lose all the test matches in South Africa, Beaumont decided it was time for a last clarion call. On the coach to a training session before the next match against the star studded South African Barbarians, he gave a short, impassioned speech, urging his men to play their hearts out for the final four games and make sure that when they walked through the terminal gates at Heathrow Airport on July 14, they would do so with their heads held high. His plea received an emphatic, positive response.

The South Africans had brought in the brilliant Argentinian fly half Hugo Porta as a guest in the Barbarians side, but even his canny breaks and elegant running could not hold back the tourists. Irvine and Tomes scored tries, and Tony Ward scored not only a try but kicked three penalties and two conversions into the bargain. The final score of a thrilling game was 25-14 to the Lions. They were back on course.

Beaumont had left himself on the bench for the Barbarians game but now he came back to inspire his troops through example against the strong Western Province at Newlands. The Lions decimated the opposition, running in three tries. Campbell was back to his best kicking form and slotted four penalties, two conversions and two fine drop goals. One to go before the finale.

Again Beaumont sat it out. He could not risk injury now, but his troops, led by Quinnell, played their hearts out for him. A close match ended with a 23-19 victory for the Lions over Griqualand West in the mining town of Kimberly though for the eighth and last time in the tour it was soured with tragedy. Colin Patterson, the first choice scrum half, damaged knee ligaments and had to be substituted by John Robbie. Robbie scored a try and a drop goal which augered well for the final test, but Patterson's injury proved severe enough to end his career at international level.

The Lions had no cover now at scrum half so Steve Smith of England was called up simply to sit on the bench. He was delighted with his long weekend, observing cheerfully that he would now become a perennial quiz question: 'name the British Lion who never played for the British Lions?' And so, after two and a half gruelling months the weary caravan arrived in Pretoria, the South African state capital, for the final showdown.

18

1980: A FINAL FLOURISH

The impressive string of victories in the run up to the
fourth test had lifted the players' spirits and convinced
Billy that they could return home with at least one test
victory to show for their efforts. Not so the press.
Those with long memories, or at least, access to the
relevant statistics, pointed out in lengthy despatches
home that no Lions side – not even Willie John
McBride's – had managed to win the last encounter.
Australia had won the fifth of five tests in 1933, but in
a dead rubber. New Zealand had won the fourth test
of four in 1928, and that was more significant because
it squared the series. But in the passage of almost fifty
years since the last achievement, touring had changed
and the pressures were now far greater. There is no
doubt that at the end of a long and gruelling tour the
players' eyes are fixed almost obsessively on the best
window seat on the plane home. There is the added
distraction of finding time to say goodbye to new
friends, buy presents, write letters. What the 1980
Lions had that perhaps the others (New Zealand
excepted) lacked was a burning determination to atone
for their failures and send their popular captain home
happy, and a hero. Even Mike Campbell Lamerton in
the disastrous tour of 1962 had been able to show one
drawn test (the first) to accompany the other three
comprehensive defeats. So it was against this
intimidating background that the Lions ran out on to
the Loftus Versfeld on Saturday July 12 for what
would be the most important game many of them
would ever play.

143

The Lions had chosen a team to do a job, to borrow current soccer parlance. The wingers, Carleton and Hay, were uncompromising defenders. The same applied to Dodge and Gravell in the centre: only the brave or the lucky would pass that line. Campbell was pleased to have Robbie rather than Patterson as his half back partner. The quicksilver Irishman had the speed of pass to give the fly half an extra yard or two advantage before Louw and the other Springbok flankers arrived. This would prove crucial because Campbell was a fine tactical reader of a game and now he was likely to have the time to take some of the options he spotted. The pack was unchanged, which meant the Springboks could expect to spend another afternoon going backwards. The only question mark in Billy's mind was – will South Africa be too lucky for us?

They nearly were. Campbell had a fine game – but not with the boot. Of eight attempts at goal he managed to land only two of them and that is an unacceptable conversion rate at this level. Yet his running was free and clever, and it was largely due to his beautifully judged changes of pace that the Lions created room in the midfield to set up O'Driscoll to drive within fingertip distance of the Springbok line. He was held up by van Heerden but he made the ball available for the prop, Clive Williams, and with the Lions pack crushing their full weight behind him, he was driven over for a try. Campbell had by then missed four penalties, so Andy Irvine, who had started the move, was called up by Beaumont to take the conversion. Sadly, he missed as well and the Lions changed ends at half time only 7-3 in the lead, Botha and Campbell having earlier exchanged penalties.

It is doubtful if an international team has ever been as comprehensively outplayed up front as the Springboks in that first forty minutes. At times, they seemed almost in a state of panic but by the same token, the Lions had apparently lost the knack of

144

creating scoring chances. They had led 7-3 in Port Elizabeth. Could the same ghastly scenario be repeated once again? There were plenty of reasons for believing it might. Soon after the restart, Botha surprised everyone by running the ball in midfield instead of booting it to the far corners of the universe. His run took him past two defenders and Willie du Plessis swerved past two more to touch down near the posts. Now it was 7-7 but, staggeringly, Botha's simple conversion was completely mis-hit. The crowd booed and jeered as the ball sailed under the bar at rather less than shoulder height. Would the magic return, or was Botha, in this match at least, a spent force? Morne du Plessis didn't wait to find out the answer. The next chance that came the Springboks' way, a fifty-five yard penalty, saw him throw the ball to full back Gysie Pienaar, so by a strange irony, the two finest goalkickers in international football had been relieved of their duties in the same match. Pienaar, though, was enjoying the kind of season others only dream about. He could do no wrong and, sure enough, he goaled the difficult penalty. And two minutes later, when the Lions got caught offside, repeated the trick. Lions 7, Springboks 13 — no one could believe it.

It was all or nothing now. Beaumont's forwards continued to win the ball at will and under his urging the backs at last began to use it constructively. Two or three thrusts into Springbok territory looked promising and Campbell was sensible enough to persevere with the tactics of letting the ball out along the line. His reward came when Hay set off on a determined run down the wing and Irvine supported him. The full back seized his chance when Hay was finally brought down, gathering the loose ball quickly and cleanly and lunging over. There were many who felt that Irvine was marginally offside, but the referee, M. Bonnet, was up with play and he ruled the try was a good one. The luck had changed for the

145

Lions at long last. With the score, Irvine equalled the world record of 210 points in international matches. Phil Bennett of Wales had been the previous holder achieving the total in nine fewer games than Irvine's 46.

At 13-10, the Lions were still worryingly behind but Beaumont insisted that only a calm, controlled approach would see them through. Build-ups must be calculated and secure. The advice was taken and duly brought its reward when the most improved player on the tour, John O'Driscoll, bulldozed his way over the line with half the Springbok pack clinging to him. Earlier, Irvine had failed to pass to Carleton when a clear overlap would surely have led to a try and saved the fingernails of many of the British supporters in the crowd. Now it was just a question of hanging on and the admirable Robbie kept play so tight at the base of the scrum that the Springboks never really got another look in. The whistle sounded, the Lions had won 17-13 and the most astonishing tour in rugby history had come to a glorious end.

19

1981: PARADISE LOST

After the high-octane atmosphere of a major overseas tour, there is bound to be some sort of let-down when domestic battle resumes. Billy found his Grand Slam team breaking up before his very eyes either through retirement or injury, and the team that set out to repeat the trick in 1981 was no better or worse than any other in the international championship. Most criteria, in fact, marked 1981 down as a season of mediocrity, and the French side that emulated England by winning the Grand Slam was rather harshly regarded as the worst ever to achieve that distinction.

Most of the Lions were slow to return to club and representative rugby at the beginning of October and some, perhaps war-weary and battle-scarred, were already considering the benefits of retirement. Before the season had ended, Fran Cotton, Roger Uttley and Tony Neary would call it a day for England, and Derek Quinnell of Wales, so able a deputy for Beaumont in South Africa, would also hang up his boots. To add to Billy's worries, the England side would suffer from injuries to key players which unbalanced the team at critical moments. And they were unlucky too, in the choice of replacements, seeming always to have the wrong one on the bench for the player injured. This was particularly evident in the opening game against Wales where Cotton tore a hamstring after fifteen minutes and was replaced by Sheppard of Bristol, tight head cover for the injury-suspect Blakeway. Sheppard packed down on the tight head and Blakeway moved into the unaccustomed position of loose head where he found himself opposing the mighty Graham Price. The England scrummage was a mess thereafter. A similar thing happened against Ireland and was decisive in transforming the match. Midway through the first half, Blakeway trapped a nerve in his neck and had to go off. This time the travelling reserve was a loose head prop, Gordon Sargent of Gloucester, so England switched their more experienced loose head Colin Smart, to tight head – and the result was a shambles. Ireland should have won. England defended a slender four point lead desperately in the last quarter of an hour, and ironically, gained a victory which put them within fingertip reach of a second Championship.

The earlier matches had seen Wales win a place kicking duel in Cardiff by 21 points to 19. Full back Dusty Hare kicked five goals for England and scored their only try, but the Welsh squeaked home via Davies' try and dropped goal, plus Fenwick's four penalties and one conversion. In a way it was poetic justice for Wales. At Twickenham in 1980 they had outplayed Beaumont's team with fourteen men after Ringer had been sent off and only suffered the indignity of defeat in the dying seconds when Hare kicked a decisive penalty. Now it was Fenwick's turn to repay the compliment, two minutes into injury time. As the ball sailed over, the Wales' captain jumped up and punched the air like a footballer who has scored the winning goal in the F.A. Cup Final at Wembley.

On the same January day in Paris, France were getting off to a solid start with a 16-9 win over Scotland. Neither side sparkled but the French showed that whatever else happened, they would be a tough side to beat. Their forward strength was formidable. France won again a fortnight later, squeaking home 19-13 in Dublin against a much improved Ireland, but the result which turned the season on its head came in Edinburgh where Scotland thoroughly outplayed Wales to win 15-6. Beaumont realised England had a lifeline back into the Championship race, and the Calcutta Cup match at Twickenham which followed was likely to be one of the pivotal matches of the season. It was in this match that England's injury jinx continued, Jeavons coming off after fourteen minutes to be replaced by Hesford of Bristol. Hesford was a Number 8 but equally at home at flanker, Jeavons's position, so the England scrummage was not disrupted this time. The only significant change in the England line-up was at fly half where the hugely promising Huw Davies made his England debut in place of the injured John Horton. He had a cracking game, scoring a try and kicking and passing beautifully. Davies was to become Player of the Year in his debut season – an unprecedented achievement.

The game was exciting and unpredictable with each side scoring three tries and only Dusty Hare's greater accuracy with his place kicking separating the teams. England finished 23-17 ahead and, sure enough, they were back in the hunt.

Wales regained momentum with a 9-8 win over Ireland in Cardiff after sending out virtually a completely new side. No less than ten changes were made, only a couple of them positional, and the biggest shock was the axing of skipper Steve Fenwick, the hero against England. Fenwick never played for his country again and later, he switched codes to Rugby League for the newly formed Cardiff Blue Dragons where he was later joined by Paul Ringer and Tommy David.

England set themselves up for a grand showdown with France at Twickenham on the last Saturday of the international season, by beating Ireland in Dublin in that injury-plagued match. It left the Irish, pre-season favourites again, alongside England, staring at a possible wooden spoon, while Wales also found their season in ruins after the new look team were turned back 19-15 by France in a bruising battle in Paris.

It was fitting that the championship should be decided at Twickenham and most pressmen gave England, back at full strength, a favourite's chance. The French, though, had an ace or two up their sleeves, notably their drop-kicking specialist at fly half, Guy Laporte. The lanky Frenchman was a 'geriatric' by international rugby standards, into his thirties and far from experienced at the top level. All doubts about Billy's own fitness had been banished. In the match against Scotland, he had received a bang on the head towards the end of the game and suffered bad concussion. Because the game was so close and England had already used their forward replacement, Hesford, Billy refused to go off and concluded the match despite having only partial vision. Most people thought it the act of a brave man – which it was. But only Billy was aware of just how brave. After the game he knew he would suffer from blinding headaches, slurred speech and numbness in one side of his body. They were symptoms he had become all too familiar with in a career that was beginning now to dish out too many bad knocks.

This was the last international that really mattered for the England captain.

The match was played on a firm pitch, but in a near gale which was to have a significant influence on the final result. Billy won the toss and elected to face the wind in the first half, a decision for which he has been criticised by the 'old timers' in the game who believe first use of the wind is a prerequisite for success. But Billy was only reflecting the views of the vast majority of players who prefer to have the advantage in the second half when the opposition are tiring. For the tactic to work, though, England would have to defend well enough to keep any French score down to manageable proportions. This they failed to do, but only just.

In the second half, England were 16 points adrift and four prodigious penalty goals by their new full back Marcus Rose almost stole the game for them. But Rose missed two others and anyway, France should not have been in such a commanding lead if referee Allan Hosie of Scotland had not made one of the worst and most significant refereeing mistakes in international rugby history.

France were in the lead in the first half through a Laporte drop goal but England were looking sound in defence. Rose, collecting a loose ball, booted mightily into touch near his own twenty-two metres line and the ball sailed into the stands to land in the lap of R.F.U. president Dickie Jeeps in the committee box. Hosie was either distracted or unaware because when Berbizier, standing on the wing, grabbed a ball from the ball boy and took a quick throw in to Rives, Hosie allowed play to go on, and Lacans dived over unopposed in the corner. It seemed that everyone but the referee was aware of the ghastly miscarriage of justice. Under the Laws, the same ball must be used, and in any case, a quick throw is only permitted if it is retrieved by the players and touched by no one else on the way. Berbizier had broken both those Laws. Billy made a mild protest which the referee noted but ignored. Had he consulted his touch judge, he would have been in a position to change his decision. But he did not and touch judges, unlike football referees, are not allowed to volunteer their views on matters concerning the Laws. If the incident had happened in a soccer game, there would surely have been a riot. As it was, England accepted the decision, albeit reluctantly, and got on with the game.

Beaumont and his team strove mightily in the second half but the French defended superbly and those four penalties by Rose were all the home side had to show for their efforts. On balance, injustice or not, England were not quite worth a win. But on the other hand, France were not worth a Grand Slam. As I say, it was not a vintage season.

When Billy looked back on the twelve months since leading the Lions on their great adventure, there were less highlights than usual. Lancashire had lost the Northern Group title to Northumberland and the Geordies had gone on to win the County Championship 15-6 against Gloucester, and in their centenary season. Compensation had come Billy's way in leading the North to a 6-0 victory over the Midlands in the final of the new Divisional Championship, but the weather at Twickenham was so 'unspeakably vile' as one writer put it that only 1000 spectators turned up to watch.

Even Fylde were less than immaculate in 1981. They put no less than 828 points on the board, one of their highest-ever totals, yet lost fifteen matches in a season which saw them finish only half way up the Northern Merit Table. They also stumbled at the semi-final stage of the Lancashire Cup and, according to Rothman's *Rugby Yearbook*, were able to call on the services of the England captain for less than half of their games. But if 1981 was disappointing for Billy, 1982 would be crushing. The knock against Scotland was a signal that the end was closing in. It didn't seem like it then but after playing against Beziers in France on a pre-season tour with Lancashire in August, even Billy must have realised he had problems.

The game in question was a friendly against a French Select XV and there were barely two minutes left when Billy, coming down after catching a high ball, received an almighty crack on the head from a French boot. It was an accident; but for Billy, a serious one. When he regained consciousness, he had more of the usual symptoms and was even taken to the local hospital at one o'clock in the morning to be examined by a local specialist. His advice, apparently, was to give up rugby! But when Billy returned to England for a second opinion, he was given the all clear by a specialist in Liverpool.

By the time the season proper got under way, Billy had forgotten all about the Beziers incident. He played for Fylde and Lancashire with his usual commitment, and the county side, now enjoying their own centenary season, were in sparkling form. It was Beaumont's ambition to captain them to the championship once more and when they duly beat Gloucestershire, 24-16 in the semi-finals, it looked as though he would have his wish. Their opponents would be North Midlands, captained by Les Cusworth of Leicester. But while Cusworth's team had bucked the odds and done well to reach their first final, no one gave them a real chance of success, despite home advantage at Moseley.

Meanwhile, the international season was under way with England opening their campaign against Scotland at Murrayfield. Most of Britain was under snow but the electric blanket under the pitch made it possible to play the game and for the Scots, at least, it was a thriller. England were leading 9-6 through penalty goals from Paul Dodge (2) and Marcus Rose. Scotland had replied with one penalty from Irvine and a fine drop goal from fly half John Rutherford. Injury time was four minutes old and the referee practically had his whistle to his lips when the England prop, Colin Smart, unaccountably barged Paxton over when he was without the ball and Scotland were awarded a penalty. Irvine placed the ball down, five yards inside his own half, and struck one of the greatest goals of even his illustrious career. The final score was 9-9. England had been robbed and they would have to begin all over again against Ireland in the next match at Twickenham.

Billy, convinced that England, had enough resources to come back and capture the title, was looking forward to the game. But of course, he never made it. The loss of vision in the County Championship final which forced him to leave the pitch – and the glory – to his team mates, spelt the end. The specialists were adamant – he must stop immediately or risk permanent injury, even death. He took the advice, realistically but reluctantly, and English rugby lost one of its greatest personalities and players.

Today, Billy has not only come to terms with his retirement, but is thriving in the exciting atmosphere of a second 'career'. He is a regular summariser on BBC Television, captains a side on the popular quiz game *A Question of Sport* and writes a regular, widely read column in *Rugby World* magazine. The only black spot, as far as he is concerned, is the fact that he is now officially 'professionalised' and until there is a change in the Laws relating to amateur status (which I predict there will be, and very soon) he is banned from coaching or administration of the game at any level – and for life. It seems a tragic waste of such a wise and experienced man. He has, of course, joined a long and distinguished line which embraces such luminaries as Gareth Edwards, David Duckham, Phil Bennett, Ian McLauchlan and Fran Cotton.

It was Fran Cotton who perhaps summed up best just what Billy had given to English rugby when he told John Taylor, the former Wales flanker, now journalist with the *Mail on Sunday*, 'He was such a genuine, honest sort of bloke. You often get captains who say all the right things, but with Billy you knew he would be the first to try and carry them out. If you see him trying that hard you've got to give a bit more yourself.'

It is a fitting epitaph. Billy gave it all.

MATCH
STATISTICS

ENGLAND CAREER RECORD 1975-1982

Year	Date	Opponents	Venue	Result
1975	1 January	Ireland	Dublin	Lost 9-12
1975	24 May	Australia	Sydney	Lost 9-16
1975	31 May	Australia	Brisbane	Lost 21-30
1976	3 January	Australia	Twickenham	Won 23-6
1976	17 January	Wales	Twickenham	Lost 9-21
1976	21 February	Scotland	Murrayfield	Lost 12-22
1976	6 March	Ireland	Twickenham	Lost 12-13
1976	20 March	France	Paris	Lost 9-30
1977	8 January	Scotland	Twickenham	Won 26-6
1977	5 February	Ireland	Dublin	Won 4-0
1977	19 February	France	Twickenham	Lost 3-4
1977	5 March	Wales	Cardiff	Lost 9-14
1978	21 January	France	Paris	Lost 6-15
1978	4 February	Wales	Twickenham	Lost 6-9
1978	4 March	Scotland	Murrayfield	Won 15-0

1978	18 March	Ireland	Twickenham	Won 15-9
1978	25 November	New Zealand	Twickenham	Lost 6-16
1979	3 February	Scotland	Twickenham	Drew 7-7
1979	17 February	Ireland	Dublin	Lost 7-12
1979	3 March	France	Twickenham	Won 7-6
1979	17 March	Wales	Cardiff	Lost 3-27
1979	24 November	New Zealand	Twickenham	Lost 9-10
1980	19 January	Ireland	Twickenham	Won 24-9
1980	2 February	France	Paris	Won 17-13
1980	16 February	Wales	Twickenham	Won 9-8
1980	15 March	Scotland	Murrayfield	Won 30-18
1981	17 January	Wales	Cardiff	Lost 19-21
1981	21 February	Scotland	Twickenham	Won 23-17
1981	7 March	Ireland	Dublin	Won 10-6
1981	21 March	France	Twickenham	Lost 12-16
1981	30 May	Argentina	Buenos Aires	Drew 19-19
1981	6 June	Argentina	Buenos Aires	Won 12-6
1982	2 January	Australia	Twickenham	Won 15-11
1982	16 January	Scotland	Murrayfield	Drew 9-9

LEADING CAP-WINNERS
(up to 30 April 1982)

ENGLAND		SCOTLAND	
A Neary	43	A B Carmichael	5
J V Pullin	42	A R Irvine	4
D J Duckham	36	J M Renwick	4
D P Rogers	34	A F McHarg	4
W B Beaumont	34	J McLauchlan	4
P J Wheeler	33	H F McLeod	4
W W Wakefield	31	D M D Rollo	4
F E Cotton	31	J MacD Bannerman	3
E Evans	30	A R Smith	3
R Cove-Smith	29	I S Smith	3
C R Jacobs	29	F A L Laidlaw	3
M P Weston	29	I R McGeechan	3
P J Squires	29	N S Bruce	3
M A C Slemen	29	I H P Laughland	3
J Butterfield	28	G L Brown	3
A T Voyce	27	W I D Elliot	2
J S Tucker	27	W M Simmers	2
C N Lowe	25	P K Stagg	2
J D Currie	25	A J Tomes	2
M S Phillips	25	J W Y Kemp	2
C B Stevens	25	K J F Scotland	2
S J Smith	25	P C Brown	2
R E G Jeeps	24	D Drysdale	2
P J Larter	24	J C McCallum	2
A G Ripley	24	G P S Macpherson	2
J MacG K Kendall-Carpenter	23	W E Maclagan	2
R W D Marques	23	J B Nelson	2
R M Uttley	23	J P Fisher	2
J P Scott	23	J W Telfer	2
W J A Davies	22	G D Stevenson	2
P E Judd	22	M A Biggar	2
C W Ralston	22	M C Morrison	2
P J Dixon	22	J A Beattie	2
J G G Birkett	21	M J Campbell-Lamerton	2
H G Periton	21	J N M Frame	2
P B Jackson	20	W C C Steele	2
N E Horton	20	B H Hay	2
P W Dodge	20	C T Deans	2

D R Bedell-Sivright	22	W E Crawford	30
A Robson	22	J D Clinch	30
S Wilson	22	J L Farrell	29
R J Arneil	22	B G M Wood	29
R G MacMillan	21	A J F O'Reilly	29
W P Scott	21	M Sugden	28
W E Kyle	21	J S McCarthy	28
J M B Scott	21	L M Magee	27
J R Patterson	21	A R Dawson	27
W B Welsh	21	M G Molloy	27
P W Kininmonth	21	J J Moloney	27
A J W Hinshelwood	21	R M Young	26
D W Morgan	21	G R Beamish	25
C Reid	20	K D Mullen	25
D S Davies	20	J C Walsh	25
J C Dykes	20	F P K Bresnihan	25
W R Logan	20	A T A Duggan	25
J C Dawson	20	B J McGann	25
J T Greenwood	20	T O Grace	25
J W C Turner	20	S A McKinney	25
N A MacEwan	20	J A E Siggins	24
D G Leslie	20	A Tedford	23
		J W McKay	23
IRELAND		F Gardiner	22
C M H Gibson	69	J A O'Meara	22
W J McBride	63	A A Mulligan	22
J F Slattery	56	M K Flynn	22
T J Kiernan	54	A H Ensor	22
J W Kyle	46	C E Allen	21
K W Kennedy	45	R Roe	21
M I Keane	43	P O'Callaghan	21
G V Stephenson	42	J C Parke	20
N A A Murphy	41	J McVicker	20
N J Henderson	40	C J Hanrahan	20
R J McLoughlin	40	D J O'Brien	20
S Millar	37	N H Brophy	20
J R Kavanagh	35	M G Doyle	20
W A Mulcahy	35		
P A Orr	35	**WALES**	
E O'D Davy	34	J P R Williams	55
W P Duggan	33	G O Edwards	53
A C Pedlow	30	T G R Davies	46
G T Hamlet	30	K J Jones	44

T M Davies	38	B L Williams	2
G Price	38	W O G Williams	2
D Williams	36	S J Dawes	2
R M Owen	35	T J Davies	2
B V Meredith	34	E M Jenkins	2
D I E Bebb	34	B Thomas	2
W D Morris	34	W R Willis	2
A J Martin	34	D Watkins	2
W J Bancroft	33	W Llewellyn	2
B Price	32	A F Harding	2
J R G Stephens	32	J Webb	2
G A D Wheel	32	A Skym	2
J J Williams	30		
S P Fenwick	30	**FRANCE**	
W J Trew	29	*NB Matches against Inter*	
C I Morgan	29	*national Board countries onl*	
P Bennett	29	R Bertranne	5
R W Windsor	28	B Dauga	5
A J Gould	27	M Crauste	4
W C Powell	27	W Spanghero	4
M C Thomas	27	J-P Lux	4
H J Morgan	27	J Prat	3
R C C Thomas	26	R Paparemborde	3
A E I Pask	26	J-P Rives	3
S J Watkins	26	M Celaya	3
J Taylor	26	A Boniface	3
G Travers	25	A Domenech	3
H Tanner	25	J-C Skréla	3
B John	25	G Dufau	3
N R Gale	25	M Vannier	3
W D Thomas	25	E Cester	3
J Squire	25	P Villepreux	2
E Gwyn Nicholls	24	C Darrouy	2
R T Gabe	24	J Dupuy	2
D J Lloyd	24	C Dourthe	2
J J Hodges	23	J Iracabal	2
E C Davey	23	J-M Aguirre	2
J A Gwilliam	23	A Cassayet	2
R H Williams	23	J Bouquet	2
J Young	23	G Basquet	2
D L Quinnell	23	A Jauréguy	2
R W R Gravell	23	R Biénès	2
T R Prosser	22	E Ribère	2

M Prat	25	**NEW ZEALAND**	
L Mias	25	C E Meads	55
J Gachassin	25	I A Kirkpatrick	39
J-P Bastiat	25	K R Tremain	38
A Paco	25	B G Williams	38
P Albaladejo	24	B J Robertson	34
C Lacaze	24	W J Whineray	32
R Bénésis	24	D B Clarke	31
J Trillo	24	S M Going	29
A Roques	23	A M Haden	29
G Boniface	23	R W Norton	27
C Carrère	23	B J Lochore	25
G Cholley	23	B E McLeod	24
M Pomathios	22	K F Gray	24
J-P Romeu	22	I J Clarke	24
M Communeau	21	S S Wilson	24
F Moncla	21	R A White	23
J-L Azarète	21	D J Graham	22
J-L Joinel	21	D Young	22
B Chevallier	20	K L Skinner	20
P Lacroix	20	C R Laidlaw	20
C Spanghero	20	I N MacEwan	20
J-L Averous	20	P J Whiting	20
SOUTH AFRICA		**AUSTRALIA**	
F C H Du Preez	38	P G Johnson	42
J H Ellis	38	A R Miller	41
J F K Marais	35	G V Davis	39
J P Engelbrecht	33	J E Thornett	37
J L Gainsford	33	J N B Hipwell	36
J T Claassen	28	A A Shaw	34
F du T Roux	27	N M Shehadie	30
L G Wilson	27	P E McLean	29
T P Bedford	25	K W Catchpole	27
D J de Villiers	25	G A Shaw	27
P J F Greyling	25	C T Burke	26
S H Nomis	25	M E Loane	26
P J Visagie	25	R B Prosser	25
D J Hopwood	22	G Cornelsen	25
A C Koch	22	J K Lenehan	24
M Du Plessis	22	J P L White	24
J A du Rand	21	J W Cole	24

161

G Fay	24	R J Heming	21
R Phelps	23	A N McGill	21
R A Smith	22	A S Cameron	20
E T Bonis	21	B J Ellwood	20
P F Hawthorne	21	C J Windon	20

ENGLAND 24 (v) IRELAND 9
Twickenham, 19 January 1980

ENGLAND   **IRELAND**

W H Hare	(Leicester)	K A O'Brien	(Broughton Park)
J Carleton	(Orrell)	T J Kennedy	(St Mary's College)
¹A M Bond	(Sale)	A R McKibbin	(London Irish)
N J Preston	(Richmond)	¹P P McNaughton	(Greystones)
M A C Slemen	(Liverpool)	A C McLennan	(Wanderers)
J P Horton	(Bath)	S O Campbell	(Old Belvedere)
S J Smith	(Sale)	C S Patterson	(Instonians)
F E Cotton	(Sale)	P A Orr	(Old Wesley)
P J Wheeler	(Leicester)	C F Fitzgerald	(St Mary's College)
†P J Blakeway	(Gloucester)	G A J McLoughlin	(Shannon)
*W B Beaumont	(Fylde)	M I Keane	(Lansdowne)
N E Horton	(Mosely)	J J Glennon	(Skerries)
R M Uttley	(Wasps)	J B O'Driscoll	(London Irish)
J P Scott	(Cardiff)	W P Duggan	(Backrock College)
A Neary	(Broughton Park)	*J F Slattery	(Blackrock College)

¹Replaced by †C R Woodward (Leicester)   ¹Replaced by I J Burns (Wanderers)

Tries: Scott, Slemen, Smith   *Penalties:* Campbell (3)
Conversions: Hare (3)
Penalties: Hare (2)

Referee: Mr C Thomas (Wales)

ENGLAND 9 (v) WALES 8
Twickenham, 16 February 1980

ENGLAND		WALES	
W H Hare	(Leicester)	W R Blyth	(Swansea)
J Carleton	(Orrell)	H E Rees	(Neath)
C R Woodward	(Leicester)	D S Richards	(Swansea)
P W Dodge	(Leicester)	S P Fenwick	(Bridgend)
M A C Slemen	(Liverpool)	L Keen	(Aberavon)
J P Horton	(Bath)	W G Davies	(Cardiff)
S J Smith	(Sale)	T D Holmes	(Cardiff)
F E Cotton	(Sale)	C Williams	(Swansea)
P J Wheeler	(Leicester)	A J Phillips	(Cardiff)
P J Blakeway	(Gloucester)	G Price	(Pontypool)
*W B Beaumont	(Fylde)	A J Martin	(Aberavon)
M J Colclough	(Angoulême)	G A D Wheel	(Swansea)
¹R M Uttley	(Wasps)	P Ringer	(Llanelli)
J P Scott	(Cardiff)	E T Butler	(Pontypool)
A Neary	(Broughton Park)	*J Squire	(Pontypool)

¹Replaced by M Rafter (Bristol)

Penalties: Hare (3)   *Tries:* Rees, Squire

Referee: Mr D I H Burnett (Ireland)

FRANCE 13 (v) ENGLAND 17
Parc des Princes, Paris, 2 February 1980

FRANCE		ENGLAND	
S Gabernet	(Toulouse)	W H Hare	(Leicester)
D Bustaffa	(Carcassonne)	J. Carleton	(Orrell)
R Bertranne	(Bagnères)	C R Woodward	(Leicester)
D Codorniou	(Narbonne)	N J Preston	(Richmond)
J L Averous	(La Voulte)	M A C Slemen	(Liverpool)
A Caussade	(Lourdes)	J P Horton	(Bath)
J Gallion	(Toulon)	S J Smith	(Sale)
P Salas	(Narbonne)	F E Cotton	(Sale)
P Dintrans	(Tarbes)	P J Wheeler	(Leicester)
R Paparemborde	(Pau)	P J Blakeway	(Gloucester)
Y Duhard	(Bagnères)	*W B Beaumont	(Fylde)
A Maleig	(Oloron)	M J Colclough	(Angoulême)
*J-P Rives	(Toulouse)	R M Uttley	(Wasps)
M Carpentier	(Lourdes)	J P Scott	(Cardiff)
J L Joinel	(Brive)	A Neary	(Broughton Park)

Tries: Averous, Rives   *Tries:* Carleton, Preston
Conversion: Caussade   *Penalty:* Hare
Penalty: Caussade   *Dropped goals:* Horton (2)

Referee: Mr C Norling (Wales)

SCOTLAND 18 (v) ENGLAND 30
Murrayfield, Edinburgh, 15 March 1980

SCOTLAND		ENGLAND	
*A R Irvine	(Heriot's FP)	W H Hare	(Leicester)
K W Robertson	(Melrose)	J Carleton	(Orrell)
J M Renwick	(Hawick)	C R Woodward	(Leicester)
D I Johnston	(Watsonians)	P W Dodge	(Leicester)
¹B H Hay	(Boroughmuir)	M A C Slemen	(Liverpool)
J Y Rutherford	(Selkirk)	J P Horton	(Bath)
R J Laidlaw	(Jedforest)	S J Smith	(Sale)
J N Burnett	(Heriot's FP)	F E Cotton	(Sale)
K G Lawrie	(Gala)	P J Wheeler	(Leicester)
N A Rowan	(Boroughmuir)	P J Blakeway	(Gloucester)
A J Tomes	(Hawick)	*W B Beaumont	(Fylde)
D Gray	(West of Scotland)	M J Colclough	(Angoulême)
D G Leslie	(Gala)	R M Uttley	(Wasps)
J R Beattie	(Glasgow Acads)	J P Scott	(Cardiff)
M A Biggar	(London Scottish)	A Neary	(Broughton Park)

¹Replaced by J S Grossman (W of Scotland)

Tries: Rutherford, Tomes
Conversions: Irvine (2)
Penalties: Irvine (2)

Tries: Carleton (3), Slemen, Smith
Conversions: Hare (2)
Penalties: Hare (2)

Referee: Mr J P Bonnet (France)

ENGLAND TO AUSTRALIA, 1975

THE TOURING PARTY

Full-backs
P E Butler (Gloucester)
A J Hignell (Cambridge U)
Threequarters
P J Squires (Harrogate)
A J Morley (Bristol)
D M Wyatt (Bedford)
P S Preece (Coventry)
K Smith (Roundhay)
A W Maxwell (New Brighton)
*J P A G Janion (Richmond)
Half-backs
W N Bennett (Bedford)
A J Wordsworth (Cambridge U)
*A G B Old (Middlesbrough)
W B Ashton (Orrell)
P Kingston (Gloucester)
*I N Orum (Roundhay)

Forwards
A G Ripley (Rosslyn Park)
D M Rollitt (Bristol)
A Neary (Broughton Park)
S R Callum (Upper Clapton)
*P J Dixon (Gosforth)
R M Uttley (Gosforth)
W B Beaumont (Fylde)
R M Wilkinson (Bedford)
N D Mantell (Rosslyn Park)
F E Cotton (Coventry)
M A Burton (Gloucester)
P J Blakeway (Gloucester)
*B G Nelmes (Cardiff)
J V Pullin (Bristol)
J A G D Raphael (Northampton)
Replacement during tour

Captain: A Neary *Manager:* A O Lewis *Assistant Manager:* J Burgess

164

TOUR RECORD

Played 8   Won 4   Lost 4   Points for 217   Against 110

MATCH DETAILS

1975	Opponents	Venue	Score
10 May	Western Australia	Perth	W 64-3
13 May	Sydney	Sydney	L 10-14
17 May	New South Wales	Sydney	W 29-24
20 May	New South Wales	Goulburn	L 13-14
24 May	AUSTRALIA	Sydney	L 9-16
27 May	Queensland	Brisbane	W 29-3
31 May	AUSTRALIA	Brisbane	L 21-30
3 June	Queensland Country	Townsville	W 42-6

MATCH 1   10 May, Perth

Western Australia 3 (1PG)   **England XV 64** (8G 3PG 1DG 1T)
Western Australia: B Smith **P**; V Robson, R Lynch, D Rosewell, R Ashley; N Gibson, T Bradbury (*capt*); *No 8* D Bennett; *Second Row* J Wilkins, D Wilson, S Henry, D Gater; *Front Row* D Commons, G Russell, D Gleghorn   *Replacements* B Mackie for Gater (65 mins), G Clark for Smith (75 mins)
England XV: Hignell; Squires **T**, Maxwell, Preece **T**, Morley **4T**; Bennett **2T, 8C, 3P, D**, Ashton; *No 8* Uttley; *Second Row* Rollitt **T**, Mantell, Wilkinson, Neary (*capt*); *Front Row* Blakeway, Pullin, Cotton
Referee L Arbuckle (Perth)

MATCH 2   13 May, Sydney

Sydney 14 (1G 2T)   **England XV 10** (1G 1T)
Sydney: R C Brown; J R Ryan **T, C**, C F Blunt, R R Andrews, L E Monaghan; K J Wright **T**, P J Carson; *No 8* G Harris; *Second Row* G K Pearse, J S King, G Fay, R A Price **T**; *Front Row* R Graham (*capt*), C M Carberry, S C Finnane   *Replacement* N Maltby for Andrews (58 mins)
England XV: Butler **C**; Squires, Preece, Smith, Wyatt **T**; Wordsworth, Kingston; *No 8* Ripley **T**; *Second Row* Callum, **Beaumont**, Uttley, Neary (*capt*); *Front Row* Burton, Raphael, Cotton   *Replacement* Blakeway for Cotton (68 mins)
Referee R G Byres (Sydney)

MATCH 3   17 May, Sydney (Sports Ground)

New South Wales 24 (1G 2PG 3T)   **England XV 29** (3G 1PG 2T)

New South Wales: R C Brown **C, 2P**; L E Monaghan **T**, R Andrews, G A Shaw, J R Ryan **T**; K J Wright, J N B Hipwell (*capt*) **T**; *No 8* A M Gelling; *Second Row* G Cornelsen, R A Smith, G Fay, R A Price; *Front Row* R Graham, P A Horton, S C Finnane **T**   *Replacement* J K Lambie for Price (51 mins)

England XV: Butler; Squires **T**, Preece **4T**, Maxwell, Morley; Bennett **P, 3C**, Kingston; *No 8* Ripley; *Second Row* Rollitt, Uttley, Mantell, Neary (*capt*); Burton, Pullin, Blakeway

Referee W M Cooney (Sydney)

MATCH 4   20 May, Goulburn

New South Wales Country 14 (1G 2T)   **England XV 13** (1G 1PG 1T)

New South Wales Country: M A Fitzgerald; D S McKinlay **T**, G A Shaw **T**, B McKay, I D Cameron **T**; J C Hindmarsh **C**, J N B Hipwell (*capt*); *No 8* A M Gelling; *Second Row* J K Lambie, G S Eisenhauer, B W Mansfield, G Cornelsen; *Front Row* J J Dawson, P A Horton, R T Leslie   *Replacements* P Prince for Gelling (53 mins), M McDougall for McKay (72 mins)

England XV: Hignell; Morley, Maxwell, Janion, Wyatt; Bennett, Orum; *No 8* Uttley; *Second Row* Callum, **Beaumont**, Wilkinson, Neary (*capt*); *Front Row* Burton, Raphael, Nelmes   *Replacement* Squires for Bennett (54 mins)

Referee G Collett (Sydney)

MATCH 5   24 May, Sydney

AUSTRALIA: R C Brown (New South Wales) **D, 2P**; L E Monaghan (New South Wales), L J Weatherstone (Australian Capital Territory), D H Osborne (Victoria); K J Wright (New South Wales) **D**, J N B Hipwell (New South Wales) (*capt*); *No 8* M E Loane (Queensland) **T**; *Second Row* A A Shaw (Queensland), R A Smith (New South Wales), G Fay (New South Wales), R A Price (New South Wales); *Front Row* S C Finnane (New South Wales), P A Horton (New South Wales), S G Macdougall (Australian Capital Territory)

ENGLAND: Butler **P, C**; Squires **T**, Janion, Maxwell, Morley; Bennett, Kingston; *No 8* Ripley; *Second Row* Rollitt, Uttley, Mantell, Neary (*capt*); *Front Row* Burton, Pullin, Nelmes   *Replacements* Wordsworth for Bennett (15 mins), **Beaumont** for Neary (23 mins)

Referee W M Cooney (Sydney)

MATCH 6 27 May, Brisbane

Queensland 3 (1PG) **England XV 29** (3G 1PG 2T)
Queensland: B Cooke; R McKay, G Shambrook, G Weeks, D Regeling; P E McLean **P**, R G Hauser; *No 8* M E Loane; *Second Row* M R Cocks (*capt*), A A Shaw, G White, M Flynn; *Front Row* D Dunworth, M E Freney, C Handy *Replacements* D Logan for Regeling (65 mins), W Andrews for Cooke (72 mins)
England XV: Hignell **3C**, **P**; Squires **T**, Janion **T**, Maxwell, Wyatt; Wordsworth, Orum; *No 8* Ripley **T**; *Second Row* Uttley, Wilkinson **T**, **Beaumont**, Rollitt; *Front Row* Burton, Pullin (*capt*), Nelmes *Replacements* Morley **T** for Maxwell (16 mins), Blakeway for Nelmes (57 mins)
Referee R T Burnett (Brisbane)

MATCH 7 31 May, Brisbane

AUSTRALIA 30 (2G 2PG 3T) **ENGLAND 21** (2G 3PG)
AUSTRALIA: R C Brown (New South Wales) **C**, **P**; L E Monaghan (New South Wales) **T**, L J Weatherstone (Australian Capital Territory) **T**, G A Shaw (Queensland), D H Osborne (Victoria); K J Wright (New South Wales) **C,P**, J N B Hipwell (New South Wales) (*capt*); *No 8* M E Loane (Queensland); *Second Row* A A Shaw (Queensland), R A Smith (New South Wales) **T**, G Fay (New South Wales) **T**, R A Price (New South Wales) **T**; *Front Row* S G Macdougall (Australian Capital Territory), P A Horton (New South Wales), R Graham (New South Wales)
ENGLAND: Hignell; Squires **T**, Janion, Preece, Morley; Old **2C**, **3P**, Kingston; *No 8* Ripley; *Second Row* Uttley **T**, **Beaumont**, Wilkinson, Rollitt; *Front Row* Burton, Pullin (*capt*), Nelmes
Referee R T Burnett (Brisbane)

MATCH 8 3 June, Townsville

Queensland Country 6 (1G) **England XV 42** (5G 3T)
Queensland Country: F McKeon **C**; R Sellwood, I McLellan, W McLaughlin, M Offner; G McVeigh, P McVeigh; *No 8* I Tomlinson **T**; *Second Row* B Kennon, D Armit (*capt*), J Holmes, B McDonald; *Front Row* B McLaughlin, D Thompson, D Crunkhorn *Replacements* R Armit for McLaughlin (64 mins), D Ingle for McLennan (78 mins)
England XV: Butler **2C**; Morley **2T**, Preece, Janion **T**, Wyatt **T**; Old (*capt*) **C**, Kingston; *No 8* Rollitt **T**; *Second Row* Dixon, Mantell **T**, Wilkinson **T**, Callum; *Front Row* Burton **T**, Raphael, Blakeway
Referee M McManus (Darling Downs)

167

ENGLAND TO THE FAR EAST, 1979

THE TOURING PARTY

Full-backs
W H Hare (Leicester)
A J Hignell (Bristol)
Threequarters
P J Squires (Harrogate)
M A C Slemen (Liverpool)
J Carleton (Orrell)
P W Dodge (Leicester)
R M Cardus (Roundhay)
A L McMillan (Gosforth)
Half-backs
W N Bennett (London Welsh)
G H Davies (Cardiff)
C J Gifford (Moseley)
I G Peck (Bedford)

Forwards
J P Scott (Cardiff)
T J Allchurch (Durham Univ)
N J C Pomphrey (Bristol)
R J Mordell (Rosslyn Park)
M Rafter (Bristol)
W B Beaumont (Fylde)
M J Colclough (Angoulême)
J L Butler (Gosforth)
C E Smart (Newport)
G S Pearce (Northampton)
R J Doubleday (Bristol)
P J Wheeler (Leicester)
J A G D Raphael (Bective Rangers)

Captain: W B Beaumont   *Manager:* D P Rogers
Assistant Manager: A M Davis

TOUR RECORD

Played 7   Won 7   Points for 270   Against 93

MATCH DETAILS

1979	Opponents	Venue	Score
10 May	Japan 'B'	Tokyo	W 36-7
13 May	JAPAN	Osaka	W 21-19
16 May	Kyushu	Fukuoka	W 80-3
20 May	JAPAN	Tokyo	W 38-18
26 May	Fiji Juniors	Lautoka	W 39-22
29 May	FIJI	Suva	W 19-7
1 June	TONGA	Nuku 'Alofa	W 37-17

APPEARANCES AND SCORERS

	App*	T	C	PG	DG	Pts		App*	T	C	PG	DG	Pts
Davies	6(1R)	–	21	6	–	60	Peck	4	1	–	–	–	4
Carleton	5	9	–	–	–	36	Colclough	3	1	–	–	–	4
Slemen	6	7	–	–	–	28	Wheeler	4	1	–	–	–	4
Hare	2	–	3	5	1	24	Butler	7(1R)	–	–	–	–	–
Squires	3	4	–	–	–	16	Doubleday	6	–	–	–	–	–
Scott	6	4	–	–	–	16	Pearce	6(1R)	–	–	–	–	–
Pomphrey	4	4	–	–	–	16	McMillan	5(1R)	–	–	–	–	–
Dodge	7(1R)	3	–	–	–	12	Smart	4(1R)	–	–	–	–	–
Cardus	4	3	–	–	–	12	Gifford	3	–	–	–	–	–
Beaumont	6	3	–	–	–	12	Mordell	3	–	–	–	–	–
Hignell	5	2	–	1	–	11	Rafter	3	–	–	–	–	–
Allchurch	4	2	–	–	–	8	Raphael	3	–	–	–	–	–
Bennett	2	1	–	1	–	7							

*Includes appearances as replacements (R).

SCORING DETAILS

For: 45T 24C 13PG 1DG 270 Pts
Against: 15T   6C   6PG 1DG   93 Pts

MATCH 1   10 May, Tokyo

Japan 'B' 7 (1PG 1T)   **England XV 36** (1G 2PG 6T)
Japan 'B': H Toshima; P Ohyama **T**, T Yajima, T Fukumoto, M Nakamura; M Sunamura **P**, J Matsumoto; *No 8* K Sejimo; *Second Row* M Sakamoto, T Konodo, K Segawa, H Takahashi; *Front Row* H Toyuda, T Hirai (*capt*), K Nakayama
England XV: Hignell **P**; Carleton **3T**, McMillan, Dodge **T**, Slemen **2T**; Bennett **P**, Peck; *No 8* Scott; *Second Row* Allchurch, **Beaumont** (*capt*), Colclough **T**, Mordell; *Front Row* Doubleday, Raphael, Smart   *Replacements* Butler for Allchurch (65 mins), Davies **C** for Bennett (80 mins)
Referee H Nonomura (Japan)

MATCH 2   13 May, Osaka

JAPAN 19 (1G 2PG 1DG 1T)   **ENGLAND XV 21** (2G 3PG)
JAPAN: N Tanifuji; S Mori (*capt*) **T**, M Fujiwara, Y Minamikawa, H Ujino; Y Matsuo **T, 2P, D**, A Ueda; *No 8* I Kobayashi **T**; *Second Row* K Toyoyama, T Hatakeyama, R Fukurodate, T Ishizuka; *Front Row* K Horaguchi, T Wada, T Yasui   *Replacement* T Kudo for Ujino (75 mins)
ENGLAND XV: Hare **2C, 3P**; Squires **T**, Cardus, Dodge, Slemen; Davies, Gifford; *No 8* Scott; *Second Row* Mordell, **Beaumont** (*capt*), Butler, Rafter; *Front Row* Pearce, Wheeler **T**, Smart
Referee C Norling (Wales)

MATCH 3   16 May, Fukuoka

Kyushu 3 (1PG)   **England XV 80** (10G 5T)
Kyushu: H Hatamoto; T Ishibashi, T Fukumoto, S Fujimura, T Kuki-
moto; T Nakamura **P**, T Tsuyama; *No 8* T Nishizuma (*capt*); S Takahira,
Y Yano, T Kitahara, H Fukushige; *Front Row* S Hamasaki, Y Moriuchi,
T Ohba
England XV: Hignell **2T**; Carleton **2T**, McMillan, Cardus **T**, Slemen **T**;
Davies **10C**, Peck **T**; *No 8* Scott **3T**; *Second Row* Pomphrey **2T**,
Beaumont (*capt*), Butler, Allchurch **T**; *Front Row* Pearce, Raphael,
Doubleday   *Replacements* Dodge for Cardus (half-time), Smart for
Pearce (65 mins)
Referee C Norling (Wales)

MATCH 4   20 May, Tokyo

JAPAN 18 (1G 3T)   **ENGLAND XV 38** (4G 2PG 2T)
JAPAN: N Tanifuji; S Mori (*capt*), T Yajima, Y Minimakawa **T**,
H Ujino; Y Matsuo **3T, C**, A Ueda; *No 8* I Kobayashi; *Second Row*
K Toyoyama, T Hatakeyama, R Fukurodate, T Ishizuka; *Front Row*
K Horaguchi, T Wada, K Nakayama   *Replacement* M Sasada for Wada
(45 mins)
ENGLAND XV: Hignell; Carleton **2T**, McMillan ,Dodge **2T**,Slemen;
Davies **4T, 2P**, Peck; *No 8* Scott; *Second Row* Pomphrey **2T**, **Beaumont**
(*capt*), Butler, Rafter; *Front Row* Pearce, Wheeler, Doubleday
Referee C Norling (Wales)

MATCH 5   26 May, Lautoka

Fiji Juniors 22 (3G 1T)   **England XV 39** (1G 2PG 1DG 6T)
Fiji Juniors: L Vuetaki **2C**; T Makatu **T**, J Ratu, K Vosailagi **2T**,
T Tuqiri **T**; R Nakiyoyo, V Vakatalai; *No 8* S Gutugutwai **C**; *Second
Row* M Driubalavu, T Daurewa, A Waqailiti, E Tuituba; *Front Row*
T Tubanitu, R Nasiga, S Navatu
England XV: Hare **2PG D**; Squires **2T**, Dodge, Cardus**T**, Carleton **T**;
Bennett **T**, Gifford; *No 8* Butler; *Second Row* Allchurch, **Beaumont**
(*capt*) **2T**, Colclough, Mordell; *Front Row* Pearce, Raphael, Doubleday
Referee J Peck (Fiji)

MATCH 6   29 May, Suva

FIJI 7 (1PG 1T)   **ENGLAND XV 19** (2G 1PG 1T)
FIJI: K Musunamasi **P**; J Kuinikoro, S Nasave, R Nayate **T**, W Gavidi;
P B Tikoisuva (*capt*), S Viriviri; *No 8* V Ratudrada; *Second Row*
I Cagilaba, N Uluvula, R Ganilau, R Qaraniqio; *Front Row* J Rauto,
A Racika, P Kina   *Replacement* E Labalaba for Gavidi (68 mins)
ENGLAND XV: Hignell; Squires **T**, Dodge, Cardus **T**, Slemen; Davies
2C, P, Peck; *No 8* Scott; *Second Row* Pomphrey, **Beaumont** (*capt*) **T**,
Butler, Rafter; *Front Row* Doubleday, Wheeler, Smart   *Replacements*
Pearce for Smart (35 mins), McMillan for Squires (65 mins)
Referee C Norling (Wales)

TONGA 17 (1G 1PG 2T)   **ENGLAND XV 37** (4G 3PG 1T)
TONGA: V Ma'ake **C**, **P**; M Taumoefolau, A Liava'a, M Finau **T**,
T Fakauho; S 'Alatini, P Ma'Afu; *No 8* V Tu'ipulotu; *Second Row*
F Valu (capt) **2T**, S Liava'a, P Mailefihi, S Hala'ufia; *Front Row* P Kiole,
P Katoa, O Hiko
ENGLAND XV: Hignell; Carleton **T**, Dodge, McMillan, Slemen **2T**;
Davies **4C**, **3P**, Gifford; *No 8* Scott **T**; *Second Row* Allchurch **T**, Butler,
Colclough, Pomphrey; *Front Row* Pearce, Wheeler (*capt*), Doubleday
Referee C Norling (Wales)

ENGLAND TO ARGENTINA, 1981

THE TOURING PARTY

Full-backs
W H Hare (Leicester)
B Patrick (Gosforth)
Threequarters
J Carleton (Orrell)
A M Swift (Swansea)
D M Trick (Bath)
C R Woodward (Leicester)
P W Dodge (Leicester)
N J Preston (Richmond)
Half-backs
J P Horton (Bath)
G H Davies (Cambridge Univ)
S J Smith (Sale)
N Melville (Wasps)

Forwards
J P Scott (Cardiff)
N C Jeavons (Moseley)
M Rafter (Bristol)
D H Cooke (Harlequins)
R J Hesford (Bristol)
W B Beaumont (Fylde)
J H Fidler (Gloucester)
S J Bainbridge (Gosforth)
G S Pearce (Northampton)
C E Smart (Newport)
P Rendall (Wasps)
C M McGregor (Angoulême)
S G F Mills (Gloucester)
A Simpson (Sale)

Captain: W B Beaumont   *Manager:* W G D Morgan
Assistant Manager: A M Davis

TOUR RECORD

All matches   Played 7   Won 6   Drawn 1   Points for 193   Against 100
International matches   Played 2   Won 1   Drawn 1   Points for 31
Against 25

SCORING DETAILS

All matches
For: 30T 17C 12PG 1DG 193 Pts
Against: 10T   6C 14PG 2DG 100 Pts

International matches
For: 4T 3C 3PG   –   31 Pts
Against: 3T 2C 1PG 2DG 25 Pts

MATCH DETAILS

1981	Opponents	Venue	Score
16 May	San Isidro Club	Buenos Aires	W 20-14
19 May	Northern Region XV	Córdoba	W 36-12
23 May	Buenos Aires Selection	Buenos Aires	W 34-25
25 May	Southern Region XV	Mar del Plata	W 47-3
30 May	ARGENTINA	Buenos Aires	D 19-19
2 June	Littoral Region XV	Rosario	W 25-21
6 June	ARGENTINA	Buenos Aires	W 12-6

Brian Patrick was top-scorer for the tour with 41 points, made up of nine conversions, five penalty goals and two tries, in only three appearances. Hare came next, with 37 points. Trick scored most tries, five, closely followed by Carleton and Davies, with four each. Carleton and Dodge both appeared in every match, seven, with Beaumont, Jeavons and Pearce one behind, at six.

MATCH 1   16 May, Ferrocarril Oeste Stadium, Buenos Aires

San Isidro Club 14 (2PG 2T)   **England XV 20** (2G 2T)
San Isidro Club *Tries:* F Aguirre, M Loffreda   *Penalty Goals:* M Loffreda (2)
England XV *Tries:* Swift (2), Carleton, Smart   *Conversions:* Hare (2)
   Team: Hare; Carleton, Dodge, Woodward, Swift; Horton, Smith; *No 8* Scott; *Second Row* Rafter, **Beaumont** (*capt*), Fidler, Jeavons; *Front Row* McGregor, Simpson, Smart

MATCH 2   19 May, Belgrano Stadium, Córdoba

Northern Region XV 12 (1G 2PG)   **England XV 36** (2G 6T)
Northern Region XV *Try:* P Bobadilla   *Conversion:* R Sauce   *Penalty Goals:* R Sauce (2)
England XV *Tries:* Davies (2), Patrick (2), Carleton, Trick, Scott, Preston   *Conversion:* Patrick (2)
   Team: Patrick; Trick, Preston, Dodge, Carleton; Davies, Melville; *No 8* Scott; *Second Row* Cooke, **Beaumont** (*capt*), Bainbridge, Hesford; *Front Row* Pearce, Mills, Rendall *Replacement* Smart for Rendall (48 mins)

MATCH 3   23 May, F C Oeste Stadium, Buenos Aires

Buenos Aires Selection 25 (1G 5PG 1T)   **England XV 34** (3G 4PG 1T)
Buenos Aires Selection *Tries:* A Courreges, F Sainz Trápaga
Conversion: G Beccar Varela   *Penalty Goals:* E Sanguinetti (4), G Beccar Varela
England XV *Tries:* Dodge (2), Swift, Hesford   *Conversions:* Hare (3)   *Penalty Goals:* Hare (4)
   Team: Hare; Carleton, Dodge, Woodward, Swift; Davies, Smith; *No 8* Scott; *Second Row* Jeavons, **Beaumont** (*capt*), Bainbridge, Cooke; *Front Row* Pearce, Mills, Smart *Replacement* Hesford for Cooke (30 mins)

172

MATCH 4   25 May, Parque Camet, Mar del Plata

Southern Region XV 3 (1PG)   **England XV 47** (6G 1PG 2T)
Southern Region XV *Penalty Goal:* V Cutuk
England XV *Tries:* Hesford, Trick (2), Dodge, Simpson, Carleton (2), Melville   *Conversions:* Patrick (6)   *Penalty Goal:* Patrick
   Team: Patrick; Trick, Preston, Dodge, Carleton; Horton, Melville; *No 8* Hesford; *Second Row* Rafter (*capt*), Bainbridge, Fidler, Jeavons; *Front Row* Pearce, Simpson, McGregor

MATCH 5   30 May, F C Oeste Stadium, Buenos Aires   1st International

ARGENTINA 19 (1G 1PG 2DG 1T)   **ENGLAND 19** (2G 1PG 1T)
ARGENTINA: D Baetti (Club Atlético Rosario); M Campo (Pueyrredón), R Madero (San Isidro Club), M Loffreda (San Isidro Club), A Cappelletti (Banco Nación); H Porta (Banco Nación) (*capt*), T R Landajo (Pueyrredón); *No 8* G Travaglini (Club Atlético San Isidro); *Second Row* T Petersen (San Isidro Club), A Iachetti (Hindu), E N Branca (CA San Isidro), E Ure (Club Universitario Buenos Aires); *Front Row* E E Rodriguez (El Tala, Córdoba), J Perez Cobo (San Isidro Club), F Morel (CA San Isidro)
Scorers *Tries:* Campo (2)   *Conversion:* Porta   *Penalty Goal:* Porta   *Dropped Goals:* Porta, Landajo
ENGLAND: Hare; Carleton, Woodward, Dodge, Swift; Davies, Smith; *No 8* Scott; *Second Row* Jeavons, **Beaumont** (*capt*), Fidler, Rafter; *Front Row* Pearce, Mills, Smart
Scorers *Tries:* Davies, Woodward (2)   *Conversions:* Hare (2) *Penalty Goal:* Hare
Referee J-P Bonnet (France)

MATCH 6   2 June, Jockey Club, Rosario

Littoral Region XV 21 (2G 3PG)   **England XV 25** (1G 4PG 1DG 1T)
Littoral Region XV *Tries:* M Dip, V Macat   *Conversions:* D Baetti (2) *Penalty Goals:* M Dip, D Baetti (2)
England XV *Tries:* Trick (2)   *Conversion:* Patrick   *Penalty Goals:* Patrick (4)   *Dropped Goal:* Horton
   Team: Patrick; Trick, Dodge, Preston, Carleton; Horton, Melville; *No 8* Hesford; *Second Row* Cooke, **Beaumont** (*capt*), Bainbridge, Jeavons; *Front Row* Pearce, Simpson, McGregor

173

ARGENTINA 6 (1G)   **ENGLAND 12** (1G 2PG)

ARGENTINA: D Baetti (Club Atlético Rosario); M Campo (Pueyrredón), R Madero (San Isidro Club), M Loffreda (San Isidro Club), A Cappelletti (Banco Nación); H Porta (Banco Nación) (*capt*), T R Landajo (Pueyrredón); *No 8* G Travaglini (CA San Isidro); *Second Row* T Petersen (San Isidro Club), A Iachetti (Hindu), E N Branca (CA San Isidro), E Ure (Club Universitario Buenos Aires); *Front Row* E E Rodriguez (El Tala, Cordóba), J Perez Cobo (San Isidro Club), F Morel (CA San Isidro) *Replacement* J P Piccardo (Hindu) for Madero (55 mins)
Scorers *Try:* Travaglini   *Conversion:* Porta

ENGLAND: Hare; Carleton, Woodward, Dodge, Swift; Davies, Smith; *No 8* Scott; *Second Row* Jeavons, **Beaumont** (*capt*), Fidler, Rafter; *Front Row* Pearce, Mills, Smart
Scorers *Try:* Davies   Conversion: Hare   *Penalty Goals:* Hare (2)
Referee J-P Bonnet (France)

174

BENNETT'S 1977 LIONS IN NEW ZEALAND
STATISTICAL SUMMARY

PERSONNEL

Position	Club and Country	Age	Height	Weight
Full-backs				
Andy Irvine	Heriot's FP and Scotland	25	5.10	12.8
Bruce Hay	Boroughmuir and Scotland	27	5.10	13.5
Wingers:				
Peter Squires	Harrogate and England	25	5.9	11.9
John J Williams	Llanelli and Wales	29	5.9	11.7
*Elgan Rees	Neath	23	5.8	12.7
Gareth Evans	Newport and Wales	23	5.11	13.11
Centres:				
Steve Fenwick	Bridgend and Wales	25	5.10	13.2
David Burcher	Newport and Wales	25	5.10	13.5
Mike Gibson	North of Ireland and Ireland	34	5.10	12.7
Ian McGeechan	Headingly and Scotland	30	5.9	11.3
Fly halves:				
Phil Bennett	Llanelli and Wales	28	5.7	11.4
John Bevan	Aberavon and Wales	29	5.8	12.8
Half-backs				
Douglas Morgan	Stewarts-Melville and Scotland	30	5.9	11.10
*Brynmor Williams	Cardiff	25	5.9½	12.7
*Alun Lewis	London Scottish	23	5.10	13.0
Number 8 forwards:				
Willie Duggan	Blackrock College and Ireland	27	6.3½	15.12

Flankers:

Tony Neary	Broughton Park and England	28	6.1	14.7
Trevor Evans	Swansea and Wales	29	6.1	14.4
Terry Cobner	Pontypool and Wales	30	6.0	14.4
Jeff Squire	Newport and Wales	25	6.3	15.7

Locks:

Gordon Brown	West of Scotland and Scotland	29	6.5	16.12
Allan Martin	Aberavon and Wales	28	6.5	16.8
Nigel Horton	Moseley and England	29	6.5	16.8
Moss Keane	Lansdowne and Ireland	28	6.4½	16.13
Bill Beaumont	**Fylde and England**	**25**	**6.3½**	**16.4**

Props:

Phil Orr	Old Wesley and Ireland	26	5.11	15.7
Clive Williams	Aberavon and Wales	28	6.0	15.8
Graham Price	Pontypool and Wales	25	6.0	15.4
Fran Cotton	Sale and England	29	6.2	16.7
Charlie Faulkner	Pontypool and Wales	33	6.0	15.8

Hookers:

Bobby Windsor	Pontypool and Wales	28	5.9	14.9
Peter Wheeler	Leicester and England	28	5.11	14.0

*An uncapped International player before the tour.

Roger Uttley (Gosforth and England) and Geoff Wheel (Swansea and Wales), on the original team, were unable to tour, being replaced by Jeff Squire and Moss Keane.

Three replacements were made during the tour. **Bill Beaumont** replaced Nigel Horton; Charlie Faulkner replaced Clive Williams and Alun Lewis replaced Brynmor Williams.

MATCH RECORD

Opponents	Venue	Score
Wairarapa-Bush	Memorial Park, Masterton	won 41-13
Hawkes Bay	McLean Park, Napier	won 13-11
Poverty Bay-East Coast	Rugby Park, Gisborne	won 25-6
Taranaki	Rugby Park, New Plymouth	won 21-13
King Country-Wanganui	The Domain, Taumarunui	won 60-9
Manawatu-Horowhenua	Showgrounds Oval, Palmerston North	won 18-12
Otago	Carisbrook, Dunedin	won 12-7
Southland	Rugby Park, Invercargill	won 20-12
New Zealand Universities	Lancaster Park Oval, Christchurch	lost 9-21
NEW ZEALAND (FIRST TEST)	Athletic Park, Wellington	lost 12-16
South Canterbury-Mid Canterbury-North Otago	Fraser Park, Timaru	won 45-6
Canterbury	Lancaster Park, Oval, Christchurch	won 14-13
West Coast-Buller	Victoria Square, Westport	won 45-0
Wellington	Athletic Park, Wellington	won 13-6
Marlborough-Nelson Bays	Lansdowne Park, Blenheim	won 40-23
NEW ZEALAND (SECOND TEST)	Lancaster Park Oval, Christchurch	won 13-9
New Zealand Maoris	Eden Park, Auckland	won 22-19
Waikato	Rugby Park, Hamilton	won 18-13
New Zealand Juniors	Athletic Park, Wellington	won 19-9
Auckland	Eden Park, Auckland	won 34-15
NEW ZEALAND (THIRD TEST)	Carisbrook, Dunedin	lost 7-19
Counties-Thames Valley	The Pukekohe Stadium, Pukekohe	won 35-10
North Auckland	Okara Park, Whangarei	won 18-7
Bay of Plenty	Rotorua International Stadium	won 23-15
NEW ZEALAND (FOURTH TEST)	Eden Park, Auckland	lost 9-10
Fiji	Buckhurst Park, Suva	lost 21-25

Record: Played 26, won 21, lost 5, for 607, against 320.

TOUR RECORD

Provincial Matches	Tries	Convs.	Pens.	Drop Goals	Total
British Isles	83	43	63	0	607
Opposition teams	34	14	46	6	320
International Matches					
British Isles	3	1	9	0	41
New Zealand	6	3	7	1	54

PLAYERS' INDIVIDUAL RECORD

	Tries	Convs.	Pens.	Drop Goals	Total
P Bennett (1st, 2nd, 3rd, 4th)	3	16	27	–	125
D Morgan (3, 4)	3	16	18	–	98
A Irvine (1, 2, 3, 4)	11	8	9	–	87
J J Williams (1, 2, 3)	10	–	–	–	40
E Rees (4)	8	–	–	–	32
M Gibson	2	2	4	–	24
G Evans (2, 3, 4)	6	–	–	–	24
P Squires (1)	5	–	–	–	20
B Hay	5	–	–	–	20
D Butcher (3)	5	–	–	–	20
S Fenwick (1, 2, 3, 4)	1	1	3	–	15
I McGeechan (1, 2, 3, 4)	3	–	–	–	12
B Williams (1, 2, 3)	3	–	–	–	12
J Squire (4)	3	–	–	–	12
T Cobner (1, 2, 3)	3	–	–	–	12
W Duggan (1, 2, 3, 4)	2	–	–	–	8
D Quinnell (2, 3)	2	–	–	–	8
W Beaumont (2, 3, 4)	2	–	–	–	8
A Martin (1)	–	–	2	–	6
J Bevan	1	–	–	–	4
G Brown (2, 3, 4)	1	–	–	–	4
P Orr (1)	1	–	–	–	4
C Williams	1	–	–	–	4
P Wheeler (2, 3, 4)	1	–	–	–	4
R Windsor (1)	1	–	–	–	4
Lions total	83	43	63	–	607
Opposition teams scored	34	14	46	6	320

The following players did not score on tour: T Evans (1); A Neary (4) N Horton, M Keane (1); F Cotton (2, 3, 4); G Price (1, 2, 3, 4); C Faulkner, A Lewis.

Figures in brackets following a player's name represent the actual tests played on tour by that player.

CAPTAINCY

Phil Bennett led the team in each of his fifteen tour appearances. In his absence Trevor Evans (in 4 matches); Terry Cobner (3); Ian McGeechan (2); Fran Cotton (1); and Tony Neary (1) were the captains.

BEAUMONT'S 1980 LIONS IN SOUTH AFRICA

STATISTICAL SUMMARY

PERSONNEL

(Statistics shown are those at time of selection)

Full-backs:	Country	Age	Height	Weight
Hay, B H (Bruce)	Scotland	29	5.10	13.7
†O'Donnell, R C (Rodney)	Ireland	23	5.10	13.2
*Irvine, A R (Andy)	Scotland	28	5.10	12.10
Wings:				
Carleton, John	England	25	5.10	13.0
Rees, H E (Elgan)	Wales	26	5.8	12.7
†Slemen, M A C (Mike)	England	28	6.1	12.0
Utility Back:				
Morgan, Peter	Wales	21	5.10	12.5
Centres:				
Gravell, R W R (Ray)	Wales	27	5.11	13.2
Renwick, J M (Jim)	Scotland	28	5.8	12.7
†Richards, D S (David)	Wales	25	5.9	11.10
Woodward, C R (Clive)	England	24	5.11	12.7
*Dodge, P W (Paul)	England	22	6.2	12.10
Fly Halves:				
Campbell, S O (Ollie)	Ireland	26	5.10	12.0
†Davies, W G (Gareth)	Wales	23	5.9	11.7
*Ward, A J P (Tony)	Ireland	25	5.7	12.7
Scrum Halves:				
†Holmes, T D (Terry)	Wales	23	6.1	13.2
Patterson, C S (Colin)	Ireland	25	5.5	11.0
*Robbie, J C (John)	Ireland	24	5.9	12.0
§Smith, S J (Steve)	England	28	5.11	13.0
Props:				
†Blakeway, P J (Phil)	England	29	5.10	16.7
Price, Graham	Wales	28	5.11	15.2
†Cotton, F E (Fran)	England	32	6.2	16.7
Williams, Clive	Wales	31	6.4	15.0
*Stephens, Ian	Wales 'B'	27	5.10	16.0
*Orr, P A (Phil)	Ireland	29	5.10	15.10

Hookers:
Phillips, A J (Alan)	Wales	24	5.11	14.4
Wheeler, P J (Peter)	England	31	5.11	13.10

Locks:
Beaumont, W B (Billy) Capt.	**England**	**28**	**6.3**	**16.0**
Colclough, M J (Maurice)	England	26	6.5	17.6
Martin, A J (Allan)	Wales	32	6.5	16.8
Tomes, A J (Alan)	Scotland	28	6.6	18.0

Flanks:
†Lane, S M (Stuart)	Wales	27	6.0	14.7
O'Driscoll, J B (John)	Ireland	26	6.2	15.2
Squire, J (Jeff)	Wales	28	6.3	15.4
Tucker, C C (Colm)	Ireland	27	6.1	15.2
*Williams, G P (Gareth)	Wales 'B'	24	6.4	15.0

No. 8s:
Beattie, J R (John)	Ireland	22	6.3	15.0
Quinnell, D L (Derek)	Wales	30	6.3	16.7

Manager:	*Asst. Manager:*	*Team Doctor:*
S Millar	N A A Murphy	Dr J Matthews

* Replacements who joined the team during the tour.

† Players who returned home during the tour.

§ Smith joined the tour two days before the final test as standby scrum-half.

MATCH RECORD

	Opponents	Score	British Isles T.	C.	P.	D.	Opponents T.	C.	P.	D.
Beat	Eastern Province	28-16	3	2	3	1	2	1	2	0
Beat	S.A.R.A. Inv. XV	28- 6	3	2	3	1	0	0	2	0
Beat	Natal	21-15	2	2	2	1	1	1	3	0
Beat	S.A. Invitation XV	22-19	2	1	4	0	1	0	5	0
Beat	Orange Free State	21-17	4	1	1	0	3	1	1	0
Beat	S.A.R. Fed. Inv. XV	15- 6	1	1	2	1	0	0	2	0
Lost to	SOUTH AFRICA	22-26	1	0	5	1	5	3	0	0
Beat	S.A. Country Dist.	27- 7	4	1	3	0	1	0	1	0
Beat	Transvaal	32-12	6	1	2	0	1	1	2	0
Beat	Eastern Transvaal	21-15	1	1	4	1	0	0	4	1
Lost to	SOUTH AFRICA	19-26	2	1	3	0	4	2	2	0
Beat	Junior Springboks	17- 6	3	1	0	1	1	1	0	0
Beat	Northern Transvaal	16- 9	2	1	2	0	1	1	0	1
Lost to	SOUTH AFRICA	10-12	1	0	2	0	1	1	1	1
Beat	S.A. Barbarians	25-14	3	2	3	0	3	1	0	0
Beat	Western Province	37- 6	3	2	4	3	0	0	2	0
Beat	Griqualand West	23-19	3	1	1	2	2	1	3	0
Beat	SOUTH AFRICA	17-13	3	1	1	0	1	0	3	0
			47	21	45	12	27	14	33	3

TOUR RECORD

	Played	Won	Lost	Drew	For	Against
Provincial Matches	14	14	0	0	333	167
International Matches	4	1	3	0	68	77
Full Tour	18	15	3	0	401	244

PLAYERS' INDIVIDUAL RECORD

	Games	Tries	Conv.	P.G.	D.G.	Pts.
O Campbell	7	-	6	13	3	60
C Woodward	11	4	5	8	1	53
A Ward	5	1	4	11	1	48
G Davies	4	1	3	7	1	34
A Irvine	8	4	-	4	1	31
M Slemen	5	5	1	-	1	25
J Renwick	11	1	2	2	1	17
J Carleton	10	3	-	-	-	12
E Rees	6	3	-	-	-	12
T Holmes	4	3	-	-	-	12
G Price	12	2	-	-	-	8
B Hay	11	2	-	-	-	8
J O'Driscoll	11	2	-	-	-	8
D Quinnell	9	2	-	-	-	8
J Beattie	8	2	-	-	-	8
P Morgan	7	1	-	-	1	7
J Robbie	7	1	-	-	1	7
C Williams	12	1	-	-	-	4
R Gravell	11	1	-	-	-	4
P Wheeler	11	1	-	-	-	4
M Colclough	11	1	-	-	-	4
J Squire	11	1	-	-	-	4
C Patterson	10	1	-	-	-	4
D Richards	7	1	-	-	-	4
A Tomes	7	1	-	-	-	4
G Williams	6	1	-	-	-	4
P Dodge	5	1	-	-	-	4
R O'Donnell	6	-	-	-	1	3
W Beaumont	**10**	**-**	**-**	**-**	**-**	**0**
C Tucker	9	-	-	-	-	0
A Martin	8	-	-	-	-	0
W Phillips	7	-	-	-	-	0
I Stephens	5	-	-	-	-	0
P Orr	5	-	-	-	-	0
F Cotton	4	-	-	-	-	0
P Blakeway	1	-	-	-	-	0
S Lane	1	-	-	-	-	0
S Smith	-	-	-	-	-	0
	-	47	21	45	12	401

RECORD OF THE MATCHES

MATCH 1   10 May, Port Elizabeth

Eastern Province 16   Lions 28 (10-21)
British Isles: B Hay; M Slemen **T**, P Morgan, R Gravell, E Rees **T**;
*G Davies **2P**, **D**, **C**, T Holmes **T**; F Cotton, P Wheeler, G Price,
†S Lane, W Beaumont (*capt*), A Martin, J Squire, J Beattie
Substitutes *J Renwick **P**, **C**; †D Quinnell
Eastern Province: J Pretorius **P**; C Heunis **T**, ‡H Lotz, D Campher **T**,
§H Potgieter; G Cowley **P**, **C**, M O'Shea; D Olivier, J Delport, J Ferreira,
A Johnson, G Human, S Burger, M van der Merwe (*capt*), N Snyman
Substitutes ‡G van Zyl, §T Kankowski
Referee S Strydom

MATCH 2   14 May, East London

S.A.R.A. Inv. XV 6   Lions 28 (13-3)
British Isles: R O'Donnell; E Rees **T**, J Renwick, C Woodward **3P**, **2C**,
D, J Carleton; D Richards, C Patterson; C Williams, A Phillips,
*P Blakeway, J O'Driscoll, A Tomes, M Colclough, C Tucker,
D Quinnell (*capt*) **2T**
Substitute *F Cotton
S.A.R.A. Inv. XV: S Mhlaba; B Sonto, T Ebersohn, H Mhlaba, T Konki;
F Prinsloo **2P**, W Speelman; H van Aswegen, E Malan, C Badenhorst,
T McGee, F Weitsz, A Poro, M Cushe (*capt*), T Burger
Referee J Smith-Belton

MATCH 3   17 May, Durban

Natal 15   Lions 21 (3-6)
British Isles: R O'Donnell; M Slemen **D**, **C**, D Richards, R Gravell,
J Carleton **T**; O Campbell **2P**, **C**, T Holmes **T**; F Cotton, P Wheeler,
G Price, C Tucker, W Beaumont (*capt*), A Martin, J Squire, J Beattie
Natal: T Cocks; C Brown **3P**, **C**, R Haarhoff, D Hoffman, L Sharp;
P Smith, P Manning; M Mortassagne **T**, D Spiers, B de Klerk, M Loane,
A Botha, H van Heerden, W Watt, W Claassen (*capt*)
Referee S W Malan

MATCH 4   21 May, Potchefstroom

S.A. Invitation 19   Lions 22 (12-10)
British Isles: B Hay; M Slemen **2T**, C Woodward **4P**, **C**, J Renwick,
E Rees; D Richards, C Patterson; C Williams, A Phillips, G Price,
G Williams, M Colclough, A Tomes, J O'Driscoll, D Quinnell (*capt*)
S.A. Invitation XV: T Cocks; N Davids, D Smith **T**, H Shields, T Konki;
R Blair **5P**, D Serfontein; P van der Merwe, W Kahts, M le Roux,
*J Meyers, J van Heerden, De V Visser, T Burger, W Claassen (*capt*)
Substitute *T Stofberg
Referee G Bezuidenhout

MATCH 5   24 May, Bloemfontein

Orange Free State 17   Lions 21 (7-0)
British Isles: P Morgan; M Slemen **2T**, J Renwick **P**, **C**, R Gravell,
J Carleton; D Richards, *T Holmes **T**; C Williams, P Wheeler **T**, G Price,
G Williams, W Beaumont (*capt*), M Colclough, J O'Driscoll, J Squire
Substitute *C Patterson
Orange Free State: G Pienaar **P**, **C**; D Jeffery **T**, J Rainsford, D Gerber **T**,
J du Toit; †De W Ras, B Wolmarans (*capt*) **T**; D Pretorius, K·Fenwick,
M le Roux, E Jansen, J Kritzinger, R Visagie, J Wessels, G Sonnekus
Substitute †D Froneman
Referee F Muller

MATCH 6   27 May, Stellenbosch

S.A.R.F. Inv. XV 6   Lions 15 (3-9)
British Isles: R O'Donnell **D**; P Morgan, D Richards, C Woodward,
J Carleton **T**; A Ward **2P**, **C**, C Patterson; *F Cotton, A Phillips,
I Stephens, J Beattie, A Tomes, A Martin, C Tucker, D Quinnell (*capt*)
Substitute *C Williams
S.A.R.F. Inv. XV: R Louw; F Davids, H Shields, C Williams, J Noble;
E Tobias **2P**, A Lategan; H van Aswegen, R Cockrell, H du Toit,
J Paarwater, H Bekker, De V Visser, W Williams, J Williams (*capt*)
Referee J Gouws

MATCH 7   31 May, Newlands

SOUTH AFRICA 26   LIONS 22 (16-9)
British Isles: R O'Donnell; M Slemen, D Richards, J Renwick,
*J Carleton; A Ward **5P**, **D**, C Patterson; C Williams, P Wheeler,
G Price **T**, J O'Driscoll, W Beaumont (*capt*), M Colclough, J Squire,
D Quinnell
Substitute *R Gravell
South Africa: G Pienaar; G Germishuys **T**, W du Plessis **T**,
D Smith, R Mordt; N Botha **3C**, D Serfontein **T**; R Prentis, W Kahts,
M le Roux, R Louw **T**, J van Heerden **T**, L Moolman, T Stofberg,
M du Plessis (*capt*)
Referee F Palmade (France)

MATCH 8   4 June, Windhoek

S.A. Country Dist. 7   Lions 27 (3-16)
British Isles: B Hay (*capt*); P Morgan, J Renwick **T**, R Gravell,
C Woodward **T**; G Davies **3P**, **C**, J Robbie; P Orr, P Wheeler, I Stephens,
C Tucker, A Tomes, A Martin, G Williams **T**, J Beattie **T**
S.A. Country Dist: S Mhlaba; *B Venter, H Shields, J Els, E Durrheim;
E Tobias **P**, J Venter; D Mather, N van Rensburg (*capt*), J Volschenk,
M Cushe, A Botha, R Meyer, J Wolfaardt, H Schrader
Substitute *C Williams **T**
Referee N Carstens

MATCH 9   7 June, Johannesburg

Transvaal 12   Lions 32 (9-19)
British Isles: A Irvine **P**; B Hay, *D Richards **T**, R Gravell, C Woodward
2T, P, C; G Davies **T**, C Patterson **T**; P Orr, P Wheeler, G Price **T**,
J. O'Driscoll, W Beaumont (*capt*), M Colclough, J Squire, D Quinnell
Substitute *J Renwick
Transvaal: †P Wilkinson; G Germishuys, W Hollander, D Maritz **T**;
J Fourie; L Barnard **2P, C**, J Minnaar; R Prentis, G Venter, J Strauss,
T Bosch, L van Vuuren, K de Klerk, C Pypers (*capt*), D Macdonald
Substitute †B Keevy
Referee F Burger

MATCH 10   10 June, Springs

Eastern Transvaal 15   Lions 21 (6-12)
British Isles: R O'Donnell; B Hay (*capt*), J Renwick, P Morgan,
J Carleton **T**; O Campbell **4P, D, C**, *T Holmes; C Williams, A Phillips,
I Stephens, C Tucker, A Tomes, A Martin, G Williams, J Beattie
Substitute *C Patterson
Eastern Transvaal: D van Rensburg; C van Zyl, E Durrheim, J Els,
L Lubbe; P Geere **4P, D**, P Grobler; T Botha, T Kloppers, B Volschenk,
K Fourie, K van Wyk, K Wentzel, M van Eeden, W Boshoff (*capt*)
Referee J Steenkamp

MATCH 11   14 June, Bloemfontein

SOUTH AFRICA 26   LIONS 19 (16-9)
BRITISH ISLES: A Irvine **P**; B Hay, R Gravell **T**, C Woodward, J
Carleton; *G Davies **2P, C**, C Patterson; C Williams, P Wheeler, G Price,
J O'Driscoll **T**, W Beaumont (*capt*), M Colclough, J Squire, D Quinnell
Substitute *O Campbell
SOUTH AFRICA: G Pienaar **T**; G Germishuys **T**, W du Plessis,
D Smith, R Mordt; N Botha **2P, 2C**, D Serfontein; R Prentis, W Kahts,
M le Roux, †R Louw **T**, K de Klerk, L Moolman, T Stofberg **T**, M du
Plessis (*capt*)
Substitute †T Burger
Referee F Palmade (France)

MATCH 12   18 June, Johannesburg

Junior Springboks 6   Lions 17 (6-3)
British Isles: *R O'Donnell; A Irvine **T**, J Renwick **D**, P Dodge **T**, E Rees
T; A Ward, J Robbie; †P Orr, A Phillips, G Price, J O'Driscoll,
A Martin, M Colclough, J Squire (*capt*), J Beattie
Substitutes *C Woodward **C**, †C Williams
Junior Springboks: T Cocks; D Jeffery, C Beck, D Gerber, D Botha;
G Cowley **C**, G Visagie; J Oberholzer, E Malan, H du Toit, B Geldenhuys
T, De V Visser, S Burger, E Jansen; W Claassen (*capt*)
Referee S Strydom

MATCH 13   21 June, Pretoria

Northern Transvaal 9   Lions 16 (0-16)
British Isles: A Irvine **2P**; B Hay, R Gravell, P Dodge, C Woodward;
O Campbell **C**, J Robbie; C Williams, P Wheeler, G Price, J O'Driscoll,
W Beaumont (*capt*), M Colclough **T**, C Tucker, J Squire **T**
Northern Transvaal: P Edwards; P van Zyl, T van der Merwe **T**, J Knox,
D Botha; N Botha (*capt*) **D, C**, T du Plessis; J Oberholzer, W Kahts,
C Badenhorst, B Geldenhuys, L Moolman, T Stofberg, T Burger, J
Marais
Referee F Burger

MATCH 14   28 June, Port Elizabeth

SOUTH AFRICA 12   LIONS 10 (3-7)
British Isles: A Irvine; B Hay **T**, R Gravell, P Dodge, C Woodward;
O Campbell **2P**, C Patterson; C Williams, P Wheeler, G Price,
J O'Driscoll, W Beaumont (*capt*), M Colclough, C Tucker, J Squire
South Africa: G Pienaar; G Germishuys **T**, W du Plessis, D Smith, R
Mordt; N Botha **P, D, C**, D Serfontein; R Prentis, *W Kahts, M le
Roux, R Louw, J van Heerden, L Moolman, T Stofberg, M du Plessis
(*capt*)
Substitute *E Malan
Referee J-P Bonnet (France)

MATCH 15   2 July, Durban

S.A. Barbarians 14   Lions 25 (6-19)
British Isles: A Irvine **T**; E Rees, J Renwick, P Morgan, J Carleton;
A Ward **3P, 2C, T**; J Robbie; P Orr, A Phillips, I Stephens, G Williams,
A Tomes **T**, A Martin, D Quinnell (*capt*), J Beattie
S.A. Barbarians: *S Mhlaba; F Davids **T**, P Oosthuizen, E Tobias, C
Williams; H Porta (Argentine) **C**, J Buchanan **T**; M Mortassagne, C
Rogers, T Lupini, J Meyers, A Markgraaff, H van Heerden, P Fourie,
M Loane (*capt*) **T**
Substitute *G Visagie
Referee G Harrison (New Zealand)

MATCH 16   5 July, Newlands

Western Province 6   Lions 37 (3-12)
British Isles: *A Irvine **T, D**; B Hay **T**, R Gravell, P Dodge, J Carleton;
O Campbell **4P, 2D, 2C**, J Robbie; C Williams, P Wheeler, G Price,
J O'Driscoll, W Beaumont (*capt*), M Colclough, C Tucker, J Squire
Substitute *C Woodward **T**
Western Province: S Naude; P Goosen, W du Plessis, T Ebersohn,
P Oosthuizen; C Beck **P**, D Serfontein **P**; H van Aswegen (*capt*), R
Cockrell, H du Toit, R Louw, H Bekker, De V Visser, D Johnson,
J Geldenhuys
Referee F Muller

MATCH 17   8 July, Kimberley
Griqualand West 19   Lions 23 (9-7)
British Isles: B Hay; P Morgan **T, D**, J Renwick, C Woodward, E Rees;
A Ward **P, C**, *C Patterson; P Orr, A Phillips, I Stephens, G Williams,
A Tomes, A Martin, D Quinnell (*capt*), J Beattie **T**
Substitute *J Robbie **T, D**
Griqualand West: G Rodwell; D Prins, J Jooste, A Gerber, H Lubbe;
K Erasmus, G Visagie **3P, C**; J Harrison, B Oehley, J Brown, T Koch **T**,
T van Tonder, P van Zyl (*capt*), P de Bruyn, C Oosthuizen **T**
Referee L Wessels

MATCH 18   12 July, Pretoria
SOUTH AFRICA 13   LIONS 17 (3-7)
British Isles: A Irvine **T**; B Hay, R Gravell, P Dodge, J Carleton;
O Campbell **P, C**, J Robbie; C Williams **T**, P Wheeler, G Price,
J O'Driscoll **T**, W Beaumont (*capt*), M Colclough, C Tucker, J Squire
South Africa: G Pienaar **2P**; G Germishuys, W du Plessis **T**,
D Smith, R Mordt; N Botha **P**, D Serfontein; R Prentis, E Malan, M le
Roux, R Louw, J van Heerden, L Moolman, T Stofberg, M du Plessis
(*capt*)
Referee J-P Bonnet (France)

Legend: Figures in parenthesis after the result is the half-time score.
T = Try; **C** = Conversion; **P** = Penalty goal; **D** = Drop goal.

SOUTH AFRICA vs. BRITISH ISLES
COMPLETE TEST MATCH RESULTS

| | | | | Analysis of Points | | | | | | |
| | | | | South Africa | | | | British Isles | | |
Year	Venue	S.A.	Result	T	C	P	D	T	C	P	D
1891	Port Elizabeth	Lost	0- 4	0	0	0	0	2	1	0	0
	Kimberley	Lost	0- 3	0	0	0	0	0	0	0	1^m
	Newlands	Lost	0- 4	0	0	0	0	2	1	0	0
1896	Port Elizabeth	Lost	0- 8	0	0	0	0	2	1	0	0
	Johannesburg	Lost	8-17	2	1	0	0	3	2	0	1
	Kimberley	Lost	3- 9	1	0	0	0	1	1	0	1
	Newlands	Won	5- 0	1	1	0	0	0	0	0	0
1903	Johannesburg	Drew	10-10	2	2	0	0	2	2	0	0
	Kimberley	Drew	0- 0	0	0	0	0	0	0	0	0
	Newlands	Won	8- 0	2	1	0	0	0	0	0	0
1910	Johannesburg	Won	14-10	4	1	0	0	2	0	0	1
	Port Elizabeth	Lost	3- 8	1	0	0	0	2	1	0	0
	Newlands	Won	21- 5	4	3	1	0	1	1	0	0

Year	Venue	Result	Score								
1924	Durban	Won	7- 3	1	0	0	1	1	0	0	0
	Johannesburg	Won	17- 0	4	1	1	0	0	0	0	0
	Port Elizabeth	Drew	3- 3	1	0	0	0	1	0	0	0
	Newlands	Won	16- 9	4	0	0	1	2	0	1	0
1938	Johannesburg	Won	26-12	4	4	2	0	0	0	4	0
	Port Elizabeth	Won	19- 3	3	2	2	0	1	0	0	0
	Newlands	Lost	16-21	3	2	1	0	4	1	1	1
1955	Johannesburg	Lost	22-23	4	2	2	0	5	4	0	0
	Newlands	Won	25- 9	7	2	0	0	2	0	1	0
	Pretoria	Lost	6- 9	0	0	2	0	1	0	1	1
	Port Elizabeth	Won	22- 8	5	2	0	1	2	1	0	0
1962	Johannesburg	Drew	3- 3	1	0	0	0	1	0	0	0
	Durban	Won	3- 0	0	0	1	0	0	0	0	0
	Newlands	Won	8- 3	1	1	1	0	0	0	0	1
	Bloemfontein	Won	34-14	6	5	2	0	3	1	1	0
1968	Pretoria	Won	25-20	3	2	4	0	1	1	5	0
	Port Elizabeth	Drew	6- 6	0	0	2	0	0	0	2	0
	Newlands	Won	11- 6	1	1	2	0	0	0	2	0
	Johannesburg	Won	19- 6	4	2	0	1	0	0	2	0
1974	Newlands	Lost	3-12	0	0	0	1	0	0	3	1
	Pretoria	Lost	9-28	0	0	2	1	5	1	1	1
	Port Elizabeth	Lost	9-26	0	0	3	0	3	1	2	2
	Johannesburg	Drew	13-13	1	0	3	0	2	1	1	0
1980	Newlands	Won	26-22	5	3	0	0	1	0	5	1
	Bloemfontein	Won	26-19	4	2	2	0	2	1	3	0
	Port Elizabeth	Won	12-10	1	1	1	1	1	0	2	0
	Pretoria	Lost	13-17	1	0	3	0	3	1	1	0

m = *Dropped goal from a mark*

COMPARATIVE RECORD:
ALL BRITISH ISLES TOURS TO SOUTH AFRICA

Year	Captain	Played	Won	Lost	Drew	For	Agst.
1891	W E Maclagan	19	19	0	0	224	1
1896	J F Hammond	21	19	1	1	310	45
1903	M C Morrison	22	11	8	3	231	138
1910	T Smyth	24	13	8	3	290	236
1924	R Cove-Smith	21	9	9	3	175	155
1938	S Walker	23	17	6	0	407	272
1955	R H Thompson	24	18	5	1	418	271
1962	A R Smith	24	15	5	4	351	208
1968	T J Kiernan	20	15	4	1	377	181
1974	W J McBride	22	21	0	1	729	207
1980	W B Beaumont	18	15	3	0	401	244

Statistics compiled by Teddy Schnapps, Honorary statistician, S.A. Rugby Football Union.

STAR BESTSELLERS

0352 309350	**WHISPERS** Dean R Koontz (GF)	1.95*
0352 310804	**ROGUE OF GOR** John Norman (Sci. Fantasy)	1.95*
0352 310413	**AFTERMATH** Roger Williams (GF)	1.60
0352 310170	**A MAN WITH A MAID** Anonymous (GF)	1.60*
0352 310928	**A MAN WITH A MAID VOL. II** Anonymous (GF)	1.60*
0352 395621	**THE STUD** Jackie Collins (GF)	1.60
0352 300701	**LOVEHEAD** Jackie Collins (GF)	1.50
0352 398663	**THE WORLD IS FULL OF DIVORCED WOMEN** Jackie Collins (GF)	1.60
0352 398752	**THE WORLD IS FULL OF MARRIED MEN** Jackie Collins (GF)	1.50
0352 311339	**THE GARMENT** Catherine Cookson (GF)	1.25
0426 163524	**HANNAH MASSEY** Catherine Cookson (GF)	1.25
0426 163605	**SLINKY JANE** Catherine Cookson (GF)	1.25
0352 310634	**THE OFFICERS' WIVES** Thomas Fleming (GF)	2.50*
0352 302720	**DELTA OF VENUS** Anais Nin (GF)	1.50*
0352 306157	**LITTLE BIRDS** Anais Nin (GF)	1.25*
0352 310359	**BITE OF THE APPLE** Molly Parkin (GF)	1.35

* Not for sale in Canada   Prices are subject to alteration

STAR BESTSELLERS

0352 300965	**LONELINESS OF THE LONG-DISTANCE RUNNER** Alan Sillitoe (GF)	1.50
0352 300981	**SATURDAY NIGHT AND SUNDAY MORNING** Alan Sillitoe (GF)	1.35
0352 310863	**BEST FRIENDS** Kelly Stearn (GF)	1.75
0352 310456	**GHOSTS OF AFRICA** William Stevenson (GF)	1.95*
0352 306351	**GOLGOTHA** John Gardner (Thriller)	1.50
0352 300078	**THE FIRST DEADLY SIN** Lawrence Sanders (Thriller)	1.95*
0352 30099X	**DIRTY HARRY** Philip Rock (Thriller)	1.25*
0352 307390	**THE GOOD THE BAD AND THE UGLY** Joe Millard (Western)	85p*
0352 305231	**CROSSFIRE TRAIL** Louis L'Amour (Western)	1.25*
0352 306750	**THE SUNSET WARRIOR** Eric Van Lustbader (Sci. Fic.)	1.75*
0352 306769	**SHALLOWS OF NIGHT** Eric Van Lustbader (Sci. Fic.)	1.75*
0352 306777	**DAI-SAN** Eric Van Lustbader (Sci. Fic.)	1.75*
0352 309237	**101 REASONS NOT TO HAVE SEX TONIGHT** I M Potent, M.D. (Humour)	1.25*
0352 396121	**BODYGUARD OF LIES** Antony Cave Brown (Gen. Non. Fic.)	2.50*
0352 310146	**THE COMPLETE CB RADIO** Richard Nichols (Gen. Non. Fic.)	2.50
0352 310731	**PERSONAL COMPUTERS** Peter Rodwell (Gen. Non. Fic.)	1.50

* Not for sale in Canada   Prices are subject to alteration

STAR Books are obtainable from many booksellers and newsagents. If you have any difficulty please send purchase price plus postage on the scale below to:-

> **Star Cash Sales**
> **P.O. Box 11**
> **Falmouth**
> **Cornwall**

OR

> **Star Book Service,**
> **G.P.O. Box 29,**
> **Douglas,**
> **Isle of Man,**
> **British Isles.**

While every effort is made to keep prices low, it is sometimes necessary to increase prices at short notice. Star Books reserve the right to show new retail prices on covers which may differ from those advertised in the text or elsewhere.

Postage and Packing Rate
UK: 45p for the first book, 20p for the second book and 14p for each additional book ordered to a maximum charge of £1.63. BFPO and EIRE: 45p for the first book, 20p for the second book, 14p per copy for the next 7 books thereafter 8p per book. Overseas: 75p for the first book and 21p per copy for each additional book.